Personality

Personality Development: A Psychoanalytic Perspective is a comprehensive overview of infant observation and personality development. Beginning with intra-utero life and going through to early adulthood, it focuses on the emotional tasks involved at each stage of development and the interplay of internal processes and external circumstances. Central importance is given to attachment and to psychoanalytic concepts, such as the Oedipal complex, separation and individuation, and the development of the capacity to think. The emotional processes are seen as 'states of mind' rather than fixed stages.

Using considerable new clinical and observational material, *Personality Development: A Psychoanalytic Perspective* will be of interest to those teaching personality development courses, as well as mental health and child care professionals.

Debbie Hindle is a consultant child and adolescent psychotherapist.

Marta Vaciago Smith is a consultant child and adolescent psychotherapist with the Community Mental Health Trust in Leeds.

Personality Development

A Psychoanalytic Perspective

Edited by Debbie Hindle and Marta Vaciago Smith

Routledge
Taylor & Francis Group

HOVE AND NEW YORK

First published 1999 by Routledge
27 Church Road, Hove, East Sussex BN3 2FA

Simultaneously published in the USA and Canada
by Routledge
711 Third Avenue, New York, NY 10017

Routledge is an imprint of the Taylor & Francis Group, an Informa business

Phototypeset in Times by Intype London Ltd

British Library Cataloguing in Publication Data
A catalogue record for this book is available from the British Library

Library of Congress Cataloguing in Publication Data
Personality development : a psychoanalytic perspective / edited by
Debbie Hindle and Marta Vaciago Smith ; with a preface by Margaret
Rustin.
      p. cm.
   Includes bibliographical references and index.
   1. Psychoanalysis. 2. Developmental psychology. 3. Personality.
   I. Hindle, Debbie, 1949–   . II. Smith, Marta Vaciago, 1944–   .
BF175.45.P47   1999
155.2´5–dc21   99–17408
                                                   CIP

ISBN 978-0-415-17958-4 (pbk)

Contents

Notes on contributors

Hamish Canham is a child and adolescent psychotherapist at the Tavistock Clinic, tutor on the Observational Studies course and on Clinical Training in Child Psychotherapy, and joint organising tutor of the Emotional Factors in Learning and Teaching courses.

Judith Edwards is a consultant child and adolescent psychotherapist working in a Family Consultation Centre and teaching child development at the Tavistock Clinic. She is currently joint editor of the *Journal of Child Psychotherapy*. Previous publications include chapters in *Autism and personality* (edited by A. Alvarez & S. Reid, Routledge, 1999), the *Handbook of child and adolescent psychotherapy: Psychoanalytic approach* (A. Horne & M. Lanyado, Routledge, 1999); and *Unwilling to school* (Berg & Nursten, Gaskill, 1996).

David Hardie is a child and adolescent psychotherapist who has worked in student health for 20 years, has taught on the Tavistock course on Counselling in Education, and on the Diploma in Student Counselling and the MSc in Counselling at Burbeck College. From 1976 to 1979 he was Head of Education at Peper Harrow Therapeutic Community.

Debbie Hindle is a consultant child and adolescent psychotherapist. She was the founding organiser of the Nottingham Infant Observation and Work Discussion course, and has worked in the public sector for many years. She currently is a visiting lecturer at the Under Fives Study Center, University of Virginia, Charlottesville.

Charlotte Jarvis is a child and adolescent psychotherapist who has specialised in work with adolescents, and has worked at the Brandon Centre for Counselling and Psychotherapy. She teaches and lectures at the Tavistock Clinic and on various other courses in Great Britain. Currently she is Director of Open Door, Hornsey Young Peoples Consultation Service.

Monica Lanyado helped to found the Child and Adolescent Psychotherapy training in Scotland and remains involved with training issues at the British Association of Psychotherapists in London. She carried out clinical research on sexually abusive behaviour in young adolescent boys at Great Ormond Street Hospital, London. She is former co-editor of the *Journal of Child Psychotherapy* and joint editor with Anne Horne of the *Handbook of child and adolescent psychotherapy: Psychoanalytic approach* (Routledge, 1999). She is currently in private practice.

Lisa Miller, consultant child and adolescent psychotherapist, is Chair of Children and Families Department, Tavistock Clinic. Her special interest is in infant observation and work with under-5s. She was formally organiser of the 'Under 5 Counselling service' at the Tavistock Clinic and is editor of the *International Journal of Infant Observation*.

Lynda Miller is a consultant psychotherapist at Enfield Child and Family Service and in the Learning Disabilities Service at the Tavistock Clinic. She has a special interest in working with adolescents.

Margaret Rustin is a consultant child psychotherapist at the Tavistock Clinic, London and has been on the senior staff of the Clinic since 1971. Since 1986 she has been Organising Tutor of the Tavistock Child Psychotherapy training and in 1993 she was elected Postgraduate Dean of the Clinic. She has co-authored with Michael Rustin *Narratives of love and loss* (1987), and co-edited *Closely observed infants* (1989) and *Psychotic states in children* (1997).

Ruth Seglow is a child and adolescent psychotherapist at the Marlborough Family Service, London, and co-editor of the *Bulletin of the Association of Child Psychotherapists*. She is a tutor on the Observational Studies course at the Tavistock Clinic and senior leader for Counselling: Aspects in Education, run jointly by the Tavistock Clinic and the University of East London.

Deborah Steiner trained as a child and adolescent psychotherapist at the Tavistock Clinic and worked for many years with children and families in child guidance. She has also trained as a psychoanalyst at the Institute of Psycho-Analysis, London.

Marta Vaciago Smith is a consultant child and adolescent psychotherapist within the Community and Mental Health Trust, Leeds. She is the course organiser and assistant senior lecturer for the masters degree in Psychoanalytical Observational Studies, Leeds University.

Preface

Margaret Rustin

The series of lectures gathered together in this book provide a fine representation of contemporary thinking about the development of the personality, viewed from a psychoanalytic perspective and growing from the clinical practice of the child and adolescent psychotherapist. The editors introduce the book with the most helpful overview. They expound two organising concepts, which serve to link the subsequent material, and which exemplify current preoccupations in psychoanalysis. First, they explore Oedipal themes, the necessary and painful encounter for the child with reality of parental sexuality and the crucial process of becoming aware of that from which we are excluded. The ways in which this triangular constellation reappears as a challenge and an opportunity for development in the process of growing up is linked to the second theme, that of the importance of learning to think about ourselves and others and to acquire a capacity for observation and reflection about our personal lives. These central ideas do indeed inform the detailed exploration of particular periods of development in the life of the child which follows.

It is impressive to realise as one goes along that the book has a sustained inner coherence based on the theoretical paradigm outlined by the editors, and yet succeeds in preserving the individual voices of its authors. The editors have clearly sought to avoid losing the tone of the original lectures, which created such a lively interchange with their audiences, and should also provide much opportunity for thought among readers. The emphasis of the writers is quite varied, and the methods chosen to bring to life the topic of each chapter are diverse. Some writers are more interested in what the traditions of infant and child observation have revealed, some are more drawn to the development of theory, some are more alert to the impact of social and cultural change, and some write primarily from careful and profound thinking about their clinical experiences. This variety leaves a lot of space for the individual reader to formulate lines of enquiry and to link the writers' ideas with personal and professional experience. One can also imagine that the book would serve as a basis for a reading group to work through systematically.

The book is a splendid offshoot of the lively growth of interest in the ideas of child psychotherapists throughout Britain and Europe and is also a timely contribution to contemporary thinking about the fundamentals of development. The story it tells of the relational basis for personality development is highly relevant reading for policy-makers troubled by evidence of difficulties in parent–child relationships. It greatly enriches the over-behaviouristic or somewhat superficial 'child-centred' accounts of development that often hold sway by its combination of sensitivity and rigour. It demonstrates the continuing fertility of psychoanalytic thinking, which is properly rooted in observation and clinical work.

Acknowledgements

We want to thank Margaret Rustin for helping us to organise the first Personality Development series of lectures and for identifying possible contributors. Her sustained interest in facilitating the development of child psychotherapy training outside London is evidenced by her Preface. Special acknowledgement needs to go to Margot Waddell who was a contributor to the first series of lectures represented in this book and an inspiration to so many of us who trained at the Tavistock Clinic. We are also grateful to Val Binney, consultant clinical psychologist, Children's Services, Sheffield for administering the course, and for the assistance given by her students and department. We also want to thank Jane Allen-Brown of the Centre for Psychotherapeutic Studies, University of Sheffield, where the course is currently held.

We would like to thank Karen Baker, senior registrar in child psychiatry, Nottingham who wrote a review of the series for the *Association of Child Psychotherapy Bulletin*, which led to the course being repeated elsewhere, Dr. Bernard Ratigan for his very helpful comments on the text, and also Amanda Waring and Tony Brodrick, who were involved in painstakingly preparing both the initial proposal for the book and the manuscript. We would also like to thank Alison Swan Parente and Sheila Hewitt for their time and attention given to reading the manuscript.

Finally we would like to thank all the contributors and the members of the course whose participation, lively discussion and requests for publication resulted in this book.

PERMISSIONS

In Chapter 2, 'Intra-uterine life and the experience of birth', we would like to thank Faber and Faber for their permission to include an extract from 'East Coker' in *Four Quartets*, published in *Collected poems* by T.S. Eliot 1905–1962, and for the same excerpt from 'East Coker' in *Four Quartets*, copyright 1940 by T.S. Eliot and renewed 1968 by Esme Valerie Eliot, reprinted by permission of Harcourt Brace & Company. Extracts from *The earliest relationship* (Brazelton & Cramer, 1991) were reproduced by permission H. Karnac (Books) Ltd.

In Chapter 4, *The toddler and the wider world*, some of the material has appeared in an earlier publication by Deborah Steiner, *Understanding your one year old*, Rosendale Press, 1992.

An earlier version of Chapter 8 was published in 1995 in *Psychoanalytic Psychotherapy*, 9, 3, entitled 'The transition to adulthood: Oedipal themes', by Lynda Miller.

We would like to thank Beta Copley and Barbara Forryan for giving us permission to use and to update The Directory of Further Learning Opportunities, previously published in *Therapeutic work with children and young people*, Cassell, 1997.

NOTE

On confidentiality

Throughout the book, all names of persons referred to have been changed and every effort has been made to disguise their identity, but not in ways that change the meaning of the observation and clinical material.

On terminology

Throughout the book the use of the term 'phantasy' refers to unconscious processes, and 'fantasy' to conscious thoughts and wishes. The term 'object' indicates a person with whom the subject has an emotional relationship and/or an internal object, which is a mental representation of the person or relationship.

When referring to an infant, child or adolescent either 'he' or 'she' may be used, but generally in the text 'he' is used unless reference is being made to a specific observational or clinical example.

Chapter 1

Introduction

Debbie Hindle and Marta Vaciago Smith

Fragments of the Rivers
It is not possible to descend twice in the same river

Heraclitus

As Heraclitus says, 'everything changes'. In this book we will see how throughout life we go on revisiting points of development, reliving conflicts and gaining new insights, which may in turn enrich our current lives. What follows is an account of what is essentially a journey, which begins within the family and continues into the wider world.

Development here is not envisaged as a linear trajectory, but as interlocking orbits forming a spiral. Nor does development take place in isolation, but in the context of relationships that may themselves be continually changing. In this book we emphasise the interplay between the internal and external world and the development of the thinking mind, which is so crucial to maintaining a sense of self. By trying to capture the uniqueness and complexity of the developing personality, the contents of the lectures also bear testimony to the way in which hope supports the journey described. Hope implies expectation and desire, underpinned by a feeling of trust. It is to such openness to trust that this book is addressed and to describing the way in which unresolved intrapsychic, interpersonal issues may be renegotiated at different stages of development. In this sense, the present becomes the crucible of past and future.

THE HISTORY OF THE COURSE

'Personality Development' is an integral part of a course entitled 'Observational Studies and the Application of Psychoanalytic Concepts to work with Children, Young People and Families' originated at the Tavistock Clinic.

This Observational Studies course has evolved over many years into both a foundation course for clinical training in child and adolescent psychotherapy, and a course in its own right, which since 1991 can be completed as a postgraduate diploma or an MA degree.

The development of the various components of the course was heavily influenced by Esther Bick and later by Martha Harris (M.H. Williams, 1987). The course addresses the needs of people undertaking work with children, adolescents and families. It is designed to foster and deepen awareness of human development and interaction, through the development of observational skills and an understanding of psychoanalytic concepts. The study of the various stages of the life cycle confers unity and a sense of continuity to the multifaceted experience of learning. The Personality Development section of the course provides a framework in which an understanding from different seminars and different fields of research may coalesce. Within the Tavistock Clinic, Margot Waddell, psychoanalyst and consultant child psychotherapist, taught personality development to nearly a generation of students and has influenced many of the contributors to this book. Her recently published book *Inside lives: Psychoanalysis and the growth of the personality*, referred to in the suggested reading list, is a testimony to her focus in this subject from the Kleinian and post-Kleinian psychoanalytic tradition.

During the last 20 years, Observational Studies courses have developed outside London, in Birmingham, Bristol, Edinburgh, Oxford, Leeds, Liverpool and Nottingham. These developments were made possible by the combined efforts of locally based child psychotherapists and visiting tutors from the Tavistock Clinic. Limited resources, however, meant that a flexible and imaginative approach was needed in order to offer more seminars. By joining forces between the courses in Leeds and Nottingham, we were able to mount a Personality Development course located in Sheffield, a midway point.

We needed to think about how best to meet the requirements

of the course and the needs of our students. We also thought it would be an enriching experience for our students to open the course to a wider professional audience. The course attracted a wide range of professionals, GPs, Health Visitors, Paediatricians, Child Psychiatrists, Community Psychiatric Nurses, Social Workers, Counsellors and Adult Psychotherapists, indicating an interest in psychoanalytic thinking and its relevance to professional work.

FORMAT OF THE COURSE

A series of seminars was designed to cover the stages from babyhood to early adulthood. Each seminar was divided into two parts: the first a lecture, the second a clinically based discussion. Although organised as a series, it was also intended that participants could attend individual lectures. Some repetition in the book reflects the fact that each lecturer had to take this into consideration. In the discussion, emphasis was placed on participation and students were encouraged to link the lectures with their own work experience. A reading list was provided for each lecture.

What could have been a fragmented series proved to have a robust structure. In relation to the Observational Studies courses, our presence in the seminars provided some continuity. Likewise, we found students kept themes from the lectures alive in other seminars. From feedback forms we learned that participants found the seminars to be surprisingly integrated. In retrospect we could see how crucial working together was to the success of the course. Only through the administrative support provided by the Clinical Psychology department in Sheffield was it possible for us to work together across the region

We were struck by how working together parallels the process of development. Development begins and continues within the medium of combined forces, a theme that will be addressed throughout this book. The success of the course was confirmed by the fact that it was re-run in the same format in Bristol, Durham, Liverpool and London.

FROM LECTURES TO CHAPTERS

In editing this book, our first aim was to preserve the spontaneity with which the lectures were delivered in the hope that the reader would be transported into the atmosphere of the course. As the lectures were pointers for further discussion, so it is hoped that reading the text will encourage further thought. The book is not intended to be a comprehensive work on personality development, rather an exposition of 'work in progress'. We envisage the book being used by a wide range of professionals, similar to those who attended the course. What cannot be included is the richness of the ensuing discussion, based on the clinical material within the text or brought by participants. It was to the discussions that both students and lecturers brought their dilemmas, often linked to the painful social, economic and political milieu that impacted on their work. The ensuing, ongoing conjunction of external circumstances with internal processes and reverberations was both liberating and empowering.

As all the contributors are child and adolescent psychotherapists, working and teaching mainly in the context of NHS Trusts, the material to which they make reference is taken from their experience. This may seem to give a particular bias to the consideration of personality development, as many examples are drawn from therapeutic work. The aim of the course, however, was to focus on *ordinary* development. Yet the more we thought about this, the more aware we were that in *ordinary* development there is a tension between moving on, standing still, and even retreating from the challenges of growth and change. Therapeutic work may best highlight those factors which facilitate and those which could interfere with development.

In this book, the emphasis is on development as a process. Although each chapter ends with a conclusion of that stage, the reader will be aware of the recapitulation of earlier stages in later stages. The metaphor of a spiral best illustrates the juxtaposition of linear time with the circularity of the internal experience that we are attempting to capture and describe.

DIFFERENT VOICES AND SHARED IDEAS

Each lecture is written by a different contributor. One of the purposes of the course was to offer participants the opportunity to hear a range of speakers, an experience otherwise not available outside London. Their contributions also stand as a reminder of the uniqueness of each individual's personality.

Because all contributors share the same clinical training, it was not surprising that the course was more coherent than we had initially expected. Their different voices formed a mosaic, as similar themes emerged, were repeated or were considered from different points of view. Central to our training is the development of observation skills, described in *Closely observed infants* (Miller, Rustin & Rustin, & Shuttleworth, 1989) and *Developments in infant observation—the Tavistock model* (Reid, 1997). The importance of attending to deep levels of human interaction and the capacity to reflect on emotional meaning and to learn from experience provides the core for ongoing work. The supporting theoretical framework is based on the writings of Freud, Klein, Bion and those in the broad arena of object relation theories. Throughout the book, ample use is made of psychoanalytic literature, which acts as a compass to guide our bearing and direction. Integral to all the contributors' thinking is a conviction about the interactive nature of growth and development. What is being described as personality development cannot be separated from the wider context of the interplay between different family members or significant others and what may be described as the family life cycle, which is in turn embedded in the social/cultural milieu.

THEORETICAL UNDERPINNING

Among the many themes elucidated in the lectures, two main themes repeatedly emerged: the significance of the Oedipal constellation and the development of a capacity to think. Taken together, they provide what we could call the scaffolding on which the personality is built. The Oedipal constellation involves the awareness and acceptance of the creative relationship between two people. From this comes the recognition of dependence, the need for sharing, and the internalisation of the combined object

that functions to strengthen and sustain the individual. Each development point brings a quantity of mental pain, as we will see
throughout the book. Whether this pain can be tolerated, modified
or evaded depends on the internal presence of a thinking object
and stands at the crossroads of development. The significance of
the work of Wilfred Bion in our thinking about development
cannot be overestimated. The question is 'How do we become
what we are?' Yet the moment we try to conceptualise this, to
capture the moment, circumstances may have changed. As Winnicott (1949/1958) says, 'All individuals are really trying to find a
new birth in which the line of their own life will not be disturbed by
a quantity of reacting greater than that which can be experienced
without a loss of the sense of continuity of personal existence'.

Oedipal development

'The entry into the Oedipus complex involves the introduction of
a distinctly new form of otherness into the mother-infant dyad
that requires a radical psychological-interpersonal reorganisation'
(Ogden, 1989). Throughout this book, almost all the contributors
consider the Oedipal situation at different ages and stages of
development. The idea that it encompasses a radical 'psychological-interpersonal reorganisation' frames our thinking about
this psychoanalytic concept. Most contributors to this book refer
to the Oedipus complex, but in Chapters 6 and 8 special reference
is made to the origins of Freud's concept and its significance to
developmental and clinical issues.

Sigmund Freud (1897/1961a) first 'discovered' the Oedipus
complex in the course of his self-analysis, as noted in a letter to
Fliess. Here he began to think about his hostile impulses towards
his father and loving impulses towards his mother. Freud elaborated his thinking about this complex in his clinical work and in
his writing (1909/1961f, 1920/1961k, 1923/1961l, 1924/1961m, 1924/
1961n, 1931/1961p), but as Laplanche and Pontalis (1973) clarify,
he nowhere gives a systematic account of the Oedipus complex.
The earliest versions of the complex were based on the simplest
ideas about the little boy's rivalry with the father for attention
and an exclusive relationship with the mother. Thoughts about the
Oedipus complex for the little girl were complicated by ideas such
as penis envy, and a lack of a fuller understanding of the female's
relation to her body and unconscious phantasies. Freud linked the

Oedipus complex to his developmental theory of sexuality and placed the resolution of the complex between the ages of 3 and 5 years. Over time, Freud 'saw in [the Oedipus complex] the convergence of universal psychological structure, unconscious personal meaning, and the influence of the power of desire emanating from the body' (Ogden, 1989). In this sense, the Oedipus complex became a cornerstone for his theory of psychoanalysis.

Klein (1926/1981) placed the Oedipus complex much earlier, in what Freud had described as the pre-Oedipal phase. Klein's interest in and work with very young children helped her to observe and hypothesise about their intricate, intense and alternating feelings of love and hate towards each parent. By placing the Oedipus complex within the first year of life, Klein linked it to the infant's apprehension of whole objects, which she described as the realisation of the separateness and independence of others. The sense in which the parents, like the infant, have an emotional life and relationships of their own is crucial to the growth of the capacity for love and concern.

The negotiation of this stage ushers in the possibility of distinguishing external reality from internal phantasy. The omnipotent phantasy of total possession of the object has to be relinquished for the acceptance of his/her separateness. Independence of the object involves the crucial recognition of its intimate relationship with another, to the exclusion of the infant. The infant has not 'created' him/herself with one parent but is the result of intercourse. To accept and benefit from the epistemophilic instinct, infants have to accept the first truth—the fact that their parents have given birth to them.

Development of a capacity to think

This book is also a testimony to something fundamental to human nature: the quest for knowledge, which is always in conflict with the desire to leave things unknown, to turn a blind eye. Klein (1930/1981) proposed that the love of knowledge, which she termed the 'epistemophilic instinct' was present from birth. At the beginning of her psychoanalytic journey, she was concerned with the inhibitions of questions about sexuality and the liberating effect the answering of those questions could have on phantasy life. 'With the term "epistemophilic" Klein creates an inseparable connection between the wish to investigate and to gain knowledge and the drive to love. One may therefore say that knowledge and emotion come to the world hand in hand' (Biran, 1997).

Initially, Freud described 'thinking' as an experimental, small-scale kind of acting, closely related to his distinction between the pleasure principle and the reality principle. In 1911, Freud (1911/1961g) wrote:

> Restraint upon motor discharge (upon action) which then becomes necessary, was provided by means of the process of thinking . . . Thinking was endowed with characteristics which made it possible for the mental apparatus to tolerate an increased tension of stimulus while the process of discharge was postponed.

In 1933, Freud (1933/1961q) wrote:

> . . . between a need and an action the ego has interposed a postponement in the form of the activity of thought . . . in that way it has dethroned the pleasure principle . . . Thinking is an experimental action carried out with small amount of energies, in the same way a general shifts small figures about on a map before setting his large bodies of troops in motion.

Here, Freud saw thought as preparatory to action.

Despite the militaristic and deterministic language, thinking was already connected with absence, frustration, loss, toleration of increased anxiety and postponement; and a bridge from frustration to satisfaction. When an individual is able to tolerate frustration, growth and search will begin as an alternative to immediate satisfaction.

Philosophy and psychology, since their respective origins, have dealt with the mystery of thought, its growth and development, and with the workings of the human mind. From metaphysics to epistemology, from Darwin to W. James, from Piaget to Vygotsky, we can turn to any of the greatest thinkers of the last century and we will find a theory of mind, encased in their more general approaches to the development of cognition. In psychoanalysis, we have to wait for Wilfred Bion to find a fundamentally revolutionary theory of thinking, which encompasses the whole of the individual's emotional experience and gathers every element of the subject's psychical life.

Fifty years after Freud's works, Bion returned to the development of thought as arising from the absence of a satisfaction; but if, in Freud, thought was a means to reducing tension and avoiding pain, for Bion, thought was required to think about one's own self, one's own pain.

Psychoanalysis has also changed considerably during these 50 years. What started as a drive theory, in which the object satisfies basic needs such as hunger, warmth and sexuality, after many mutations in theoretical views became an object-relations theory, in which the object is sought to satisfy the need for intimacy and dependent love. The language of psychoanalysis changed concurrently, and mechanistic terminology was superseded by words imbued with relational meanings. Klein's legacy identified the aim of the mature individual as needing to bear the pain of loss, and the responsibility for one's own emotions.

Masterfully, Bion built on the Kleinian body of theories and from his view of human endeavour. 'Thinking' became thirst for knowledge, seeking truth, the truth of one's own feelings as food for the mind. In *Learning from experience*, Bion (1962) wrote, 'Failure to use the emotional experience produces a comparable disaster in the development of the personality; I include amongst these disasters degrees of psychotic deterioration that could be described as death of the personality'. Bion's greatest legacy was the indissoluble connection, from birth, of physical, intellectual and emotional experience. The capacity to meet basic needs and to process emotional experiences, originally a function of the carer, needs to be gradually introjected by the infant. Such mental apparatus is firmly described as the tool by which emotional experience is transformed into thought.

The momentous step in the development of thought when the infant has to come to terms with the absent object is described by Bion (1962). The hungry infant in need of the breast is aware of a need not satisfied. What he experiences is the pain of his hunger, initially felt as a 'bad breast present'.

> The infant has to advance from experiencing the needed absent breast in the phantasy of a bad breast present, to being able to *think of* the real missing good breast . . . it is only by tolerating the pain and terrors of his frustrations enough that he can put himself in the position of being able to think about

them, to think, eventually that what he needs is the missing good breast.

O'Shaughnessy, 1964

Thinking is then to remain in contact with the absence of the object as absence, and to keep an object alive in the mind when absent. Such capacity can only develop if aided by the thinking mind of an adult carer who helps the still frail infant to cope with the onrush of bodily and protomental sensations. In the end, the responsibility to make use of the developing capacity for thought lies with the individual. Each individual may then use their thinking capacities to learn, establish relationships and express their creativity, or to avoid the pain of thinking, to attack learning, linking and creativity. The way in which each individual manages the tension between the desire to think and the wish to avoid the pain involved is perhaps a lifelong struggle.

The capacity to tolerate the absence of the good nurturing object is also the forerunner to introjection of such an object in the internal world. Introjection, a term coined by Ferenczi (1909), is now used to describe 'one of the most important mechanisms used to build up a secure personality through the experience of having good objects introjected and safely located inside, with the ensuing experience of an internal sense of goodness, or self-confidence and mental stability' (Hinshelwood, 1991). As a consequence of this, our internal world becomes populated by an array of good and bad objects, relationships and experiences that form the bedrock of what we call personality.

The social context

In the lectures, the contributors make reference to the social context in which individuals grow and develop, but the focus is primarily on internal processes enlightened by a psychoanalytic perspective. Although a fuller consideration of the social context is not within the scope of this book, we cannot ignore the context in which we live. In the late 1990s, on the cusp of the millennium, we are witnessing a period of rapid change, not only in Western society. Economic, social and political pressures all influence how we see ourselves, our position in relation to society and our capacity to realise our hopes and aspirations.

In the context of thinking about personality development, the family plays a central role in the care, nurture and education of children. The position of the family as an institution is perhaps more fluid than it has ever been. Several contributors mention the special pressures on single parents and the difficulties generated by separation, divorce and remarriage. The dislocation of extended families, lack of economic stability as well as migration, all fuel a sense of insecurity. Some children, for different and perhaps complex reasons, may not be able to live with their families of origin, but instead with extended family, with foster parents or become members of new families in adoptive homes. Although it is not possible to attend in detail to the special circumstances and needs of these children, how they tackle each development stage described will be affected by their cumulative experience. Separation and loss, whether through natural circumstances such as the death of a parent or carer, abuse or neglect necessitating removal of the child to ensure his or her safety and development, can have a profound impact on a child's sense of self, and on their capacity to form new attachments.

By the end of our book, our hypothetical young person has left home or is poised on the brink of leaving home. Although the last two lectures concentrate on the move to further education as one way of leaving home, we are anxious to point out that this is not the whole story, nor does it address the wider issues of the majority of young people who remain living at home while working, or those who establish separate lives with partners or friends. The problem of getting a foothold in the working world and having opportunities to acquire skills is increasingly difficult for young people. For some, unemployment further narrows their options and their hopes for the future. For others, the pull towards delinquency with its accompanying excitement, or towards drugs that dull or mask other preoccupations may become enticing or habitual alternatives. The multiplicity of possible lifestyles is not a matter for moral judgement, but an undeniable fact of our society. It is, however, the primacy of inner life, the capacity to maintain a sense of self in the face of external changes and pressure that is central to our thinking.

It is often difficult to gain a perspective on the social context in which we live or to understand its profound impact on us. The extent to which we feel ourselves to be at the mercy of these changes and uncertainty, and the extent to which they can be faced and accommodated, rather than ignored or denied, has its roots in our personality.

Note to reader

It is our intention that this book can be read sequentially, or that each lecture can stand in its own right, much as the lectures would be attended as a series or individually. For a fuller description of psychoanalytic terms used in the text, we suggest the reader refers to the references specifically noted in the 'Selected Reading List'.

Chapter 2

Intra-uterine life and the experience of birth

Ruth Seglow and Hamish Canham

'In my beginning is my end,' wrote T. S. Eliot (1963), in the *Four Quartets*. This phrase reflects the dual focus of this chapter—the start of new life in the womb and preparing to be and becoming parents.

In this lecture this complicated area is considered from different perspectives. From the perspective of the foetus, what happens during the 9 months inside the womb? From the perspective of the parents, what are some of the psychological implications of preparing for birth and parenthood? Modern research techniques such as ultrasound have made it possible for us to know more directly what goes on inside the womb, but much remains unknown. What follows is, of necessity, a brief journey around a huge subject.

ANTICIPATING PARENTHOOD—FACING THE UNKNOWN

The drive to have children is, at one level, the same drive that motivates all creatures to continue their species. Within that basic drive, the unconscious motivations between individuals for desiring or having children are many and varied. A child may be desired in order to patch up a rocky relationship, one partner may feel that a baby will keep them company, or a baby may be wanted to achieve unfulfilled parental ambitions. People may be motivated to have children in order to do things differently from their own parents, or because they feel more benignly identified with the positive aspects of their own parents. Perhaps some of us hope to leave aspects of ourselves behind when we are dead.

While individual motivations may be more or less syntonic with the responsibilities of becoming a parent, it seems important to make a distinction between physically having a baby, and having the emotional maturity to be a parent. Being a parent relies on a more adult aspect of the personality. Having a baby can be driven by any number of more or less unconscious phantasies. During the 9 months of pregnancy, while the foetus is growing, there is an opportunity for commensurate growth in the personality, which can enable an adult to become a parent.

Becoming a parent, in more or less conscious ways, puts people in touch both with their own childhood and their parents. This looking backwards and forwards, so strong at this particular point in life, is a key aspect in the development of the personality. A developmental push forward, however, is only possible if a previous phase of life can be mourned and worked through. The 9 months during which a baby is inside the womb gives parents the chance to mourn the lives they will shortly be giving up, both as individuals and as a couple. The degree to which a couple share the same motivation for wanting to start a family can play an important role in determining its success. In order to parent well, they need to recognise and contain their own infantile needs and allow the adult part of them to come to the fore.

Preparing for parenthood is therefore often a period of working through intense ambivalent feelings. Much has now been written on this subject from the point of view of both mother and father (Holloway & Featherstone, 1997). Ambivalence is aroused because although a baby may be very much desired, it also means giving up a great deal in terms of independence, money, leisure time and time spent both alone and together as a couple. The mother who is pleased to have a growing bump may also be sad to be losing her figure. The parents who have enjoyed regularly meeting up with friends may feel some resentment about feeling less able to do this once the baby is born. For both parents, pregnancy means the prospect of becoming a family, of making room in their relationship to accommodate a third person, and necessitates giving up a life in which both could think only about themselves and each other.

Brazelton and Cramer (1991) write:

> Each woman's pregnancy reflects her whole life prior to conception. Her experiences with her own mother and father, her

subsequent experiences with the Oedipal triangle, and the forces that led her to adapt to it more or less successfully and finally separate from her parents, all influence her adjustment to this new role.

It is clear that powerful unconscious forces are at work that affect a woman's attitude to her pregnancy and to the birth of her child.

The common division of pregnancy into trimesters, corresponding to a particular stage of development of the foetus, is helpful in thinking about particular anxieties associated with each stage. The first stage is taken up with the parents' response to the news of the pregnancy and to the new idea of becoming a parent. There may as yet be no observable changes in the mother's body, yet she is often experiencing new physical sensations and battling with extreme tiredness. The mother's first awareness of the baby's fluttering movements within the womb heralds in the second stage, where the parents begin to recognise the foetus as a separate being with a life of its own. In the final trimester the parents come to see the foetus as an individual who plays a part in shaping their fantasies by its own particular style of activity within the womb. As Raphael-Leff (1993) remarks 'over the three trimesters, the focus shifts from pregnancy, to foetus, to baby'.

THE FIRST TRIMESTER

Although the parents' first reaction to pregnancy is often one of delight, this may soon be tempered by the sober realisation that their lives will undergo an irrevocable change, that this change brings with it heavy responsibilities and that their one-to-one relationship will have to accommodate a third person. Reactions differ according to the significance of the pregnancy for the parents: the teenager who has become pregnant by accident will have a very different response from the middle-aged woman who has had several miscarriages. The single mother of a first baby will have different preoccupations from a married woman with an existing family. Internal and external circumstances combine to shape the experience of pregnancy. These circumstances, influenced by the parents' own life histories, are almost always surrounded by ambivalence of various kinds. 'I'm thrilled to be pregnant, but John thinks it's happened at the wrong time', 'We're both delighted but at the same time I'm already dreading giving up work and being at home all day', and 'We were both so pleased but now I find I'm terrified of having a girl and making all the same mistakes my mother made with me', are examples that highlight common reactions to the news.

Ambivalence can be extended to others outside the parental couple. A 4-year-old boy who had longed for a sibling suddenly burst out crying one day as he eyed his mother's swelling belly and sobbed, 'I don't like sharing. I want you and Daddy to myself'. A grandmother whose daughter was her only child, on hearing the news of her daughter's second pregnancy, said sharply, 'Haven't you got enough with one?' Sometimes outright hostility can be directed at the pregnant mother. A work colleague, returning from a long absence abroad to her colleague's unexpectedly enlarged abdomen, remarked dryly, 'You've been eating a lot while I've been away'.

With thoughts of future responsibilities, the serious emotional work of pregnancy begins. As Brazelton and Cramer (1991) write:

> The prospect of parenthood throws adults back to their own childhood. No adult looks back on childhood as an unmitigated pleasure. The struggles of growing up are mobilised each time an adolescent or young adult faces a crisis and, in pregnancy, these struggles are raw once again. The first fantasy of most parents-to-be is one of avoiding the struggles of their own childhood and of becoming perfect parents.

Wanting to be a good parent and to avoid the mistakes felt to have been made by one's own parents can be undertaken in two very different frames of mind. On the one hand there can be a feeling of triumphing over the parents by doing everything so much better than they did. On the other is a more benign recognition of the difficulties involved in being a parent and the gratitude to one's own parents for doing their best.

Sometimes the foetus can, in phantasy, be cast in a particular role by one or more of its parents, or even grandparents. For some children born after a miscarriage or the death of another child, the term 'replacement child' indicates that there may not have been sufficient opportunity to mourn the previous loss. The hopes, fears and expectations for the new child may be unrealistic, or coloured by unresolved feelings about the previous child. It can then be difficult or impossible for the parent to see the child as they really are, with their own particular attributes. Fraiberg's (1980) phrase 'ghosts in the nursery', serves as a metaphor for unresolved conflicts in the family's past or within a parent that casts a shadow over their perception and experience of their child. In this situation, the child can come to represent not only a previously lost child, but the parents' own childhood self or aspects of their parents, which affect the nature of the parent–child relationship in this new generation.

As we have said, in the first trimester comes the realisation that the couple will need to expand to include a third person. Negotiating a three-person relationship, with its possibilities for the exclusion of one of the parties, sets the scene for what is considered, in psychoanalytic theory, to be one of the fundamentals for the healthy growth of the personality—the working through of the Oedipus complex. It is a term used to illustrate the universal difficulty that children have in allowing their parents to exist as a couple, and for there to be aspects of the parental relationship from which they are excluded. It is a difficulty that is revisited in slightly different ways throughout life. Although normally viewed from the perspective of the child, the residues of unresolved difficulties also exist for parents. Feelings of exclusion and jealousy may parallel different pairings, graphically expressed in comments such as 'mummy's boy' or 'daddy's girl'. How each parent has resolved Oedipal issues may have an impact on the family as a whole and may in turn influence the personality development of their child.

A new baby means reconfiguring the family structure for all members. Children become parents, parents become grandparents, and the generations all move up one stage. At a time when a new birth is announced, people are paradoxically put in touch with being nearer death. The facts of life are brought into sharp focus. Money-Kyrle (1968/1978b) has written about how many of us expend considerable energy evading the facts of life: that we are the product of a union between our parents, that we are born utterly dependent, and that all of us will eventually die. The announcement that a baby is expected confronts everyone with these facts of life and contributes to the intensity of emotional feeling at this time. Life and death is a theme that remains uppermost in the minds of parents-to-be. There is often a surge of joy and sense of pride in having created a new life, but this is tempered by anxieties about whether the foetus will survive and also fears, with the coming birth, about the mother's own survival.

With one in every four pregnancies ending in miscarriage, most commonly within the first trimester, it is not surprising that the announcement of a pregnancy may be postponed until the first 12 weeks are over. Miscarriage can be a deeply upsetting experience to a newly pregnant mother, and to a father too, with the shattering of all the hopes and expectations that had been invested in the baby since conception. Some women who have miscarried report a sense of total failure, and those who were awaiting their first child may question whether they will ever become a mother at all. One woman expressed it as feeling that in relation to her own mother, she was still only a little girl after all. Groups that exist to support women who miscarry can, if sensitively run, do an enormous amount to help mothers recognise the widespread nature of this experience rather than leaving them feeling singled out for this particular disaster.

Klauber (1998, personal communication) has commented that, at the time when parents need to feel most grown-up, they often feel most like babies themselves—full of uncertainties and doubts about their capacities. Anxiety about being up to the job runs through the pregnancy. These states of mind, however, are actually necessary. Parents need to be in touch with what it feels like to be a baby, so that their more adult aspect can respond appropriately. It is a sign of maturity to be able to *feel* like a baby, yet not be so overwhelmed by it that one becomes *like* a baby.

THE SECOND TRIMESTER

As the baby's existence is confirmed both by its movements inside the mother and by the woman's changing physical appearance, the baby starts to become more of a person to its parents. They often start to fantasise about what sex it might be, consider names, and begin to ascribe to it a personality. In one mother's second pregnancy her baby was particularly lively, often kicking for long periods with great vigour, and sometimes seeming to drum on her abdominal wall with its fists. This was in great contrast to her first baby, who had been rather peaceful in utero. Her husband, regarding her heaving abdomen with alarm during one of these bursts of vigorous activity, exclaimed, 'This one's going to be hyperactive!'

Fantasising about the foetus' gender can have both helpful and unhelpful aspects. It can be a way for each parent to get in touch with their masculine and feminine sides as they imagine what it would be like to look after a boy or a girl. If, however, a particular sex is desired—say, a boy—and in fantasy that is what is imagined, the consequences for the development of the personality can be complicated if in fact the foetus turns out to be a girl. Once born, the baby may pick up on her parents' desires to have a boy, emphasise those attributes that she perceives to be masculine, and downplay her femininity. In this way the true nature or personality of the child is influenced by parental expectations, because the real gender of the child is not recognised.

The development of the personality is dependent on the interplay of the foetus' nature and personality with that of his or her parents. Growth of individuality relies on parents recognising the real foetus and baby they have—not the one they may have wished they had. Therefore, the second trimester marks the beginning of a process of moulding or accommodation. The fantasising that takes place in the parents' minds during pregnancy allows them to explore the many types of baby they could have, and prepares them for their baby's arrival.

Although technological advances in viewing and testing the health of the foetus can be hugely reassuring to parents and professionals alike, these can, as Raphael-Leff (1993) points out, 'puncture the bubble of imaginings' and prematurely present a reality that can interrupt the process of the parents' fantasy work. In a study quoted by Brazelton and Cramer (1991), Elizabeth Keller compared parents who were told the sex of their baby after amniocentesis or ultrasound with parents who waited until the birth. She found that parents who had pre-knowledge of their baby's sex took longer to personify and recognise the individuality of their babies. Keller surmised that the foresight of such facts could hinder the later reality work of attachment, and also highlighted the difficulties in adjusting to a premature baby where the fantasy work had not yet been completed.

By the second trimester, the foetus starts to make its presence felt for the first time and by the quickening within the womb makes its first contribution to the relationship with his or her parents—the mother in particular. It is an exciting and reassuring moment, providing concrete evidence of a live baby-to-be inside, yet the mother now has to face the fact of sharing her body with a being who is separate and beyond her control. The movement of the foetus inside the womb can leave fathers feeling excluded; jealous of not being able to produce babies like women whilst simultaneously feeling proud and excited by their part in its creation.

Women often feel a sense of vigour and well-being during this stage of pregnancy, when the frequent nausea and extreme tiredness of the early stage has receded. Some mothers gain new energy by being able to relate more easily to rewarding aspects of their relationships with their own mothers. Mothers or fathers whose dependency needs are too great can experience their foetuses, and later their babies, as rivals, and may treat them as envied younger siblings.

Members of the wider family may also experience the potential birth of a new baby as puzzlingly threatening. Recall the grandmother who at first sharply reproved her daughter for her second pregnancy. Later in this pregnancy, when the grandmother visited, she would watch her 5-year-old grandson interacting with her daughter and notice certain thoughts going through her head, such as 'Ah, but will she be so nice to him once the baby's born?' Although she was aware these thoughts were at odds with her experience of her daughter, it was only after much introspection that she realised she was in touch with her own sibling jealousy of an adored younger brother.

For other mothers, or fathers, who may have experienced loss or deprivation in their own childhoods, the wish for a baby to love and care for may be at odds with their own unfulfilled infantile needs. For example, a young woman of 15 became pregnant by a much older man. She had spent a greater part of her life in foster care and children's homes after having been severely neglected by her own mother. During her pregnancy, she talked of wanting to give her baby the kind of love and attention she felt she never received. When the baby was born, she found she was furious when he cried and she was not able to look after him and love him as she had hoped. Having a baby seemed motivated by a desire to rework some aspects of her own childhood, but caring for the baby powerfully evoked the neglected baby she felt herself to be. In this situation, parenting became a burden and a frustration of her own unmet needs.

The presence of a foetus inside a woman can also put a father in touch with deep longings to bear a child. Psychoanalytic theory is famous for its concept of penis envy, where girls and women wish to have the male genital they do not possess. Less well known is the idea originating with Klein (1928/1981b), the corresponding envy of women's capacity for creating, bearing and breast-feeding children. Kraemer (1991) described the impact of this dynamic in shaping the male psyche and that of fathers in particular. Considering the social implications of intra-psychic processes, Kraemer argued that it is man's destructive envy of woman's maternal capacities that led to the attempted male domination of women in the domestic, political and religious institutions of some societies.

Fantasies about an abnormal infant continue during this period so that by the time of the birth, many mothers have mentally rehearsed every kind of possible infant abnormality. If the infant is premature or impaired in some way, it can often come as less of a shock than a disappointment, but may also be a confirmation of their worst fears. The need then to grieve the loss of the perfect baby they had hoped for and to come to know and understand their own baby may be a significant task for new parents. Whether a parent recoils from a vulnerable, ill or deformed baby or responds with sympathy, concern and determination may vary. For many, the immediate feelings of disappointment, or perhaps rage, gradually give way as the parents became familiar with *their* baby. Coming to terms with his or her imperfections can also deepen their love for a baby who may need more than average time and attention. At the same time, feelings of ambivalence, concerns about extended dependency, and the demands of a handicapped or ill child may be ongoing.

THE THIRD TRIMESTER

During the final trimester of pregnancy, parents begin to adjust their external lives to accommodate the imminent arrival of their baby. As a consequence, the foetus is seen as increasingly separate and increasingly real. By this stage, many parents are already treating the foetus as a member of the family, including him in conversations, talking to him directly, watching his movements in the bed or bath, and having a physical relationship by touching the now well-defined contours of limbs. What used to be normal pre-pregnancy life becomes impossible as the woman is increasingly weighed down and slowed down by her large belly.

This adjustment in the external environment is matched by one in the internal lives of the parents. Modern technology has meant that a foetus born at any time during this stage is probably viable. Parents are confronted by the inevitability of the birth of their child, and the reality that must be faced, although many parents do not buy equipment until this stage because of the still-dominant anxiety that things could go wrong. They begin to rearrange the home to accommodate the newborn baby, to accumulate equipment and make contingency plans for childcare and leave from work or study if necessary.

This final phase is often dominated by preoccupations with the birth and about the momentous and irreversible changes that are about to occur. This is especially marked with first-time parents, where the mother in particular may seize a final opportunity to tie up loose ends or participate in social events that will all too soon be unavailable to her. The preparations the parents have made are as though they are creating a nest for the baby to replace the 'nest' of the mother's womb.

Ante-natal classes run by hospitals, the National Childbirth Trust and other groups help mothers and fathers to prepare for the birth and care of the newborn by focusing on practical details. Just as important is the function that these groups serve in providing a forum for expectant parents to share their excitement and anxieties and get to know and form a network with other parents. These classes are perhaps particularly helpful in including fathers at a time when they can feel somewhat on the periphery.

FATHERS

What of the particular emotional struggles experienced by fathers-to-be? Whereas women often feel admitted into an informal club of pregnant women and other mothers, and undergo physical and emotional changes that are with them every moment of the day and night, men are excluded from such experiences. The man looks and feels physically just the same as always. Nobody can see the fluctuations of his states of mind. Although it is often important to a man to have public proof of his virility, which his partner's pregnancy provides, he can also feel intensely resentful at having to take a back seat, as if his role in the creative process is over, and the pregnancy can proceed without him.

We have already mentioned the Oedipal difficulties that confront couples—these may be more marked for the man at this time. One aspect of the father-to-be's exclusion is the difficulty in admitting a third person to his relationship with his partner—allowing the dyad to become a triangle. As she turns inwards to her experience of her baby he may feel that mother and baby have now become the 'real' partnership, and that he is no more than a spare part. This sense of displacement can relate back to childhood experiences and fantasies when he may have felt displaced in his mother's affections by his father or a sibling. For these reasons a man is also bound to have ambivalent feelings about the baby to come.

Some men flee from the stirring-up of these feelings and withdraw, ignoring what is going on and preferring to take on extra work, spending time with male colleagues and friends perhaps, or even resorting to extra-marital affairs or bouts of heavy drinking. Other men may become impotent, withdrawing in fear from the mysterious contents of their partners' wombs. When a man is used to being the focus of his partner's attentions, having to take second place can arouse violent feelings in him about his influence being eroded, and can lead to destructive behaviour designed to re-establish his sense of masculine authority and power.

One male expression of identification with, as well as hostility to, the pregnant mother and the foetus is through the 'couvade'. In some Third World cultures the prospective father exhibits symptoms of pregnancy and labour, but in modern-day Western society the man may suffer a variety of aches and pains that call attention to himself and away from his wife, thus expressing not only his rivalry with her but often very real feelings of envy at his wife's creative abilities. It has been shown that expectant fathers experience more nausea, vomiting, gastro-intestinal disturbances and toothaches than do non-expectant men.

These symptoms may also be an expression of the father's identification with the pregnant mother and the foetus. Boys' as well as girls' first relationship is with the mother, and little boys as well as little girls play at being pregnant and stick a cushion up their jumper. In pregnancy the reviving of a boy's early identification with his mother can be expressed either by empathy with his partner or by symptoms where old, unconscious conflicts need to be understood and resolved.

In the last part of pregnancy, just as a woman may turn to the early bond with her own mother, a man may gain new interest in his relationship with his father. Brazelton and Cramer (1991) write:

> A man who enjoys a solid bond with his father is protected against fears of becoming too much like his mother.

Part of developing into parents is the realisation that the struggles and anxieties that you are undergoing are those that your own parents might have undergone with you. This is true for both men and women and can forge a closer bond between generations at this time.

It is clear that the process of pregnancy, delivery and the postpartum period is much affected by the father's attitude; a father's presence and loving support helps a woman to develop her maternal role, and it has been shown that with paternal involvement there are fewer complications and interventions in the birth process. A father who is able to tolerate the feelings of exclusion from the intimacy of the mother-baby relationship provides an important model for both his partner and child. The presence of a third person who can bear to be left out helps the young child to tolerate being excluded from certain aspects of the parental relationship. It also helps the mother and baby through the process of weaning when the closeness of the mother–infant bond loosens, and neither mother nor baby enjoy any longer such an exclusive relationship with one another.

THE FOETUS

The foetus' story through the 9 months of pregnancy to birth is the story of the journey from one world to another, from a life of water and weightlessness to a life of air and gravity. We now know that this enclosed world is far from silent. Not only do the mother's heartbeats, the coursing of her blood and the gurglings of her digestive system provide a reassuring backdrop to the weightless world of the 'foetal astronaut', as it has been called, but from the sixth month of pregnancy the foetus can hear, somewhat muffled, sounds of the outside world coming through. Newborns are attuned to the sound of their mother's voice, and recognise it post-natally, preferring it to the sound of other women's voices. Even more remarkably it has been shown that babies remember this voice and prefer stories read in utero to new ones. The voices of father and siblings too become familiar. Pieces of music that have been played repeatedly during pregnancy are recognised post-birth. One mother, in her sixth month of pregnancy, was at a jazz concert, and found her foetus apparently leaping each time the drummer played a riff. The foetus is also affected by the mother's behaviour and state of mind. Valman and Pearson (1980) report that when the mother is under emotional stress or is tired, foetal activity increases. Foetal movement can increase up to 10 times normal levels if the period of stress is protracted.

These are influences on the foetus but the foetus itself is also well able to interact with its environment. By the second trimester of pregnancy, all human senses are operative; the foetus can see, hear, taste and respond to heat and cold, to pain and to kinaes-thetic and vestibular (balance) stimuli. In addition the foetus can move to increase his or her own comfort, and it is the foetus who determines the timing of the onset of labour (Liley, 1972).

During early pregnancy the foetus moves a great deal, some-times performing incredible somersaults and pirouettes. This is now thought to contribute to the healthy development of foetal muscles, bones and joints. By 12 weeks the foetus can, and often does, suck its thumb and by the fourth month the foetus is ingesting and excreting quantities of the amniotic fluid in prep-aration for future digestion. If a sweet substance like saccharine is injected into the amniotic fluid the baby's rate of swallowing doubles. The foetus also responds to intrusive experiences and pain. During an amniocentesis one mother was relieved to observe on the screen that as the long needle was carefully introduced into her uterus to remove a sample of amniotic fluid, her baby retreated from it up into a safe corner of the womb. Brazelton and Cramer (1991) describe a series of experiments that show that the foetus in the last trimester responds reliably to visual, auditory and kinaesthetic stimulation:

> When a bright light is shone on the mother's abdomen in the fetus' line of vision, it will startle. If a softer light is used in the same position, the infant turns actively but smoothly toward it. A loud noise next to the abdomen will also produce

a startle, while if a soft noise is used, the baby will turn toward it.

By the sixth month it appears that foetuses dream; fibre-optic filming has revealed rapid eye movement similar to those of dreaming adults. Raphael-Leff (1993) speculates that foetuses may use dream time, like adults, to digest and integrate waking experiences.

By the seventh month internal organs are well developed, the foetus has finger- and toe-nails and the lungs are becoming capable of breathing air. Sexual differentiation of boys and girls, apparent since the twelfth week, is becoming complete. The rapidly enlarging foetus is increasingly restricted in its formerly spacious home and many movements are made in search of a more comfortable position. In the final trimester a mother can often distinguish between her baby's different states of alertness; between deep sleep, light sleep, active awake or an alert but quiet state.

One of the most interesting studies of intra-uterine life and its continuity with life outside the womb has been made by Piontelli (1992). She acquired evidence which seems to suggest that foetuses may be profoundly affected by their pre-natal experiences and by the state of mind of their mother during the pregnancy. Piontelli used ultrasound scans to observe 11 foetuses—3 singleton pregnancies and 4 sets of twins—monthly 5 or 6 times, from about the sixteenth week of pregnancy until just before their birth. She then observed the babies weekly, post-birth, until they were a year old, then monthly until the age of 2, and then 2 or 3 times a year until the age of 4. She found that each foetus had characteristic ways of behaving, which were to some extent and in some form or other continued in post-natal life. Of the ultrasound observations, Piontelli (1992) reports:

> What struck me was the richness and the complexity of movements one could observe right from the early stages. Long before their mothers could perceive any of these movements their babies could suck, scratch, yawn, rub their hands and feet . . . . As my experience developed I was more and more struck by the individuality of movement of each foetus and by their preferred postures and reactions . . . each of them already seemed to be an individual with its own personality, preferences and reactions. Each foetus also seemed to relate

differently to its own environment and the various components that went to make it up.

What had initially provoked Piontelli to this intra-uterine research, and in particular to the study of twins, was a therapeutic consultation she had given to the parents of an 18-month old boy she called Jacob. The parents complained of his constant restlessness and inability to sleep. During the consultation, Piontelli noted that Jacob seemed to be obsessively searching for something he could not find. Sometimes he would shake objects in her room 'as if trying to bring them back to life'. When Piontelli commented on this, Jacob's parents, close to tears, reported that in fact Jacob had been a twin, but that his brother had died in utero 2 weeks before their birth. This meant that for 2 weeks Jacob had lived with his dead and consequently unresponsive twin. Piontelli says:

> The simple realization of this, as well as the verbalization of his fears that each step forward in development, starting from the first warning signs of his imminent birth, might have been accompanied by the death of a loved one for whom he felt himself to be responsible, brought about an almost incredible change in his behaviour.

Piontelli says that infantile amnesia—the forgetting in adulthood of one's early life and the time spent in utero—used to be regarded as evidence that there was no differentiated experience early on and gave rise to the image of the blind, deaf, unfeeling neonate. This is in sharp contrast to the picture we have now of a sophisticated environment in utero and a competent neonate. Piontelli provides detailed accounts of the pre- and post-natal developments of the babies she observed. Three of her remarkable observations shed light on the development of the personality in utero.

She cites the example of Giulia, a singleton pregnancy, who was observed in utero to be continually licking the umbilical cord and the placenta and gulping quantities of amniotic fluid. After she was born Giulia continued with her preference for wildly licking her mother's chest rather than sucking at the nipple. When she finally did feed she always gulped the milk down in no time at all—just as had been observed in utero with the amniotic fluid—and then settled down to her pleasurable licking again. Her sensuousness extended to other areas, just as in the womb she was observed to prefer keeping her hands between her legs.

One set of twins—Alice and Luca—were characterised as the 'gentle twins' since they both tried to make contact with and explore each other through the dividing membrane in utero. A favourite game when they were 1 year old was to use a curtain rather like a dividing membrane while they hid on either side of it, 'then Luca would put his hand through the curtain and Alice would reach out with her head and their mutual stroking would begin, accompanied by gurgles and smiles'.

Marisa and Beatrice, in contrast, kicked and punched each other in the womb and their intense rivalry continued afterwards, both seeming to resent having half of what they could have had if they had not had to share their living space and their mother from the first.

Coleridge (1802/1992) wrote: 'The history of man for the nine months preceding his birth would probably be far more interesting and contain events of greater moment than all the three score and ten years that follow it'. This opinion grows in weight as we continue to discover more about the intra-uterine world—what Piontelli calls 'the pre-natal past'.

BIRTH AND COMPLICATIONS AROUND BIRTH

Birth is a dramatic moment for all concerned. The baby must almost immediately draw air into its lungs or perish, and thus discovers what it is to be a separate being. The mother labours hard to give up the baby inside her, and to expel it out into the world. The couple must now work together to take on the awesome responsibilities of parenthood.

Brazelton and Cramer (1991) describe the tasks that face the new mother as follows:

1 Managing the abrupt ending of the sense of fusion with the foetus, of the fantasies of completeness and omnipotence fostered by pregnancy.
2 Adapting to a new being who provokes feelings of strangeness.
3 Mourning for the imaginary (perfect) child and adapting to the characteristics of her specific baby.
4 Coping with fears of harming the helpless child (often experi-

enced in new mothers, for instance, as the fear of drowning the baby in the bath).
5 Learning to tolerate and enjoy the enormous demands made on her by the total dependency of the baby.

The circumstances of the birth and the setting also significantly influence the mother's relationship with her new baby. How long was labour? Was it in the more intimate home setting or in the more formal, medical atmosphere of a hospital? Was the mother's partner or a close friend or relative able to be with her? Was delivery straightforward or were mother and baby drowsy with drugs? Were there technological interventions of any kind? Was it a vaginal or a Caesarian delivery? Were the midwife and any other professionals present sympathetic to and supportive of the mother's and father's wishes concerning the birth? These kinds of factors make important contributions to the sort of start mother and baby will have together in the outside world. If there is a sensitive birth attendant who listens to and respects the mother's wishes and tries to facilitate the style of delivery that she wants, then a woman is helped to become a mother.

Watching his partner suffer great pain is also very difficult for a man to tolerate and causes its own stress. One husband was so put off by the unexpected and extreme difficulties that his wife encountered in giving birth to their first child (although the baby itself was healthy) that it took some years, more than had been planned, before the memories faded and he felt able to risk another pregnancy.

Sometimes, of course, things do go wrong. Very early labour can result in a late miscarriage—particularly traumatic when the mother has felt her baby alive and kicking—or in a premature birth. Sometimes the pregnancy reaches term and the baby is stillborn or handicapped in some way. These are all tragic events marked by the sudden and severe loss of all the hopes invested in the idea of a perfect baby. The mother in particular may be riddled with feelings of failure and doubt about her capacity to produce a healthy baby. Crucial work has been done by Bourne and Lewis (1992) to help change the former practices of 'tidying away' a dead baby. Seeing and holding the baby are now recognised as facilitating the process of mourning. As Raphael-Leff (1993) says: 'Only a loss that is experienced can be mourned'. When a baby is born with a defect, mourning also needs to take place for the loss of the imagined healthy baby. The parents will need a great deal of help from sensitive professionals in all these situations to think about and process the impact on them of their loss. The professionals will also need support in order to think about the impact on them of these tragic events and not to minimise them as being 'only part of the work'. If there are siblings they too will need help with mourning their loss, which comes at a time when parents can be too preoccupied with their own feelings to be able to take on board those of their existing children. Helping their children to acknowledge and understand their grief can also help the parents face what has happened, and how it affects the whole family.

There is increasingly more understanding too of babies' emotional needs when they are born prematurely. Klaus and Kennell (1982) have done pioneering work in this field, for instance, placing the baby on a fleece or on mother's bare abdomen can have more beneficial effects than being left in an unyielding incubator. Premature babies need less oxygen from a machine and can breathe more independently when held for periods in human arms. But also it has to be remembered that in utero babies are not yet ready for social interaction. When a baby is very premature—what Gesell (1945/1988) has called a 'foetal infant'—this has to be taken into account. Trying to interact with these babies by smiling or talking can overwhelm them with unwelcome stimuli. They have to be given *appropriate* stimuli. Nurses report that in later life some premature babies dislike holding hands because of the frequent drawing of blood samples they have had to suffer, or walk in an odd way because of frequent heel-prickings for the same purpose. It is important to look at these 'memories in feeling' because they can provide much evidence to help avoid more physical and emotional pain than is necessary and help us respond more appropriately to the pain that is unavoidable. McFadyen (1994) and Negri (1994), through their detailed observational and research work, have both contributed significantly to our understanding of the emotional needs of mothers and babies in this most vulnerable and stressful of situations, and have humanised an area that can easily be taken over by the medical and technological aspects of the care these babies need.

Even when birth goes well and the baby is normal, the events of labour and birth provide a gigantic upheaval for mother and baby in both a physical and an emotional sense. It is perhaps to be expected, then, that most mothers of newborns will feel emotionally vulnerable and weepy a few days after the birth. Some women cry for the loss of their inside baby and for the 9 months in which they felt so special. All women have to face the massive adjustment to providing full-time care of a tiny being utterly dependent on them. The importance of a partner's support and sharing of the responsibility at this time cannot be overestimated.

Some new mothers suffer more than 'baby blues', and may be described as having post-natal depression. There are external circumstances as well as internal ones that precipitate its onset. A re-evoking of childhood difficulties, and in particular the woman's own experience of being parented, is often found to be linked to this depression. Not surprisingly, perhaps, an absent or unsupportive father is an important factor contributing to a new mother's depression, whilst a nurturing rather than a competitive father can make all the difference to the resolution of the depression. According to Daws (1996), post-natal depression does not only *cause* relationship difficulties, it may also be the *result* of them, and the cure to it is also through relationships, professional or otherwise. The provision of a network of other mothers with babies and pregnant women is enormously helpful in this situation, and can provide tremendous support, and even transform, the lives of women with post-natal depression, thus helping to set their babies on the road to better mental and emotional health.

Birth marks the end of a particular 9-month period in which rapid emotional growth takes place for parents and foetus alike. We should not, therefore, be surprised that feelings run high for everyone in the immediate post-partum period as the struggle to adapt to a new life begins.

CONCLUSION

At the point of becoming a parent, we are closest physically to the mysterious processes that take place between two adults to create a new life and the growth of a new human being inside the mother. Preoccupations about these processes remain with us throughout life. In this lecture, we consider the factors that motivate people to want children, the feelings raised on realising conception has taken place and the complicated physical changes and emotional adjustments necessary to prepare for the arrival of a new baby. The parallel processes for the father and the parents are explored in relation to the three trimesters of pregnancy. The personality of the infant is shaped by his or her parents, but equally, the type of parents we become is significantly affected by the personality of our children and by the children we once were. As Freud (1925/1961o) wrote: 'There is much more continuity between intra-uterine life and earliest infancy than the impressive caesura of the act of birth would have us believe.'

Chapter 3

Babyhood: Becoming a person in the family

Lisa Miller

From birth, and perhaps even from before birth, there is a constant interplay between what the baby is offered and what the baby makes of it. Considering how responsive premature infants are, it is reasonable to suppose that during those last weeks in the womb a baby is a sentient being, even one who can, in some sense, experience being born.

There is a highly significant change that has to be negotiated at this point. Inside the mother, the baby is plugged into another person's system; certain essential needs are automatically met. But with the dramatic separation of birth, the baby embarks upon an autonomous existence and from the start has to make its own contribution to its own survival.

From the moment of the first breath, the baby is interacting with the world. Each baby is unique and each is faced with unique circumstances; but even where babies' initial experiences are roughly similar, their reactions can differ greatly. These reactions have an effect upon the people around them, so that what a baby does influences how it is handled and treated. Cursory observation of newborns shows how different they are: some very collected and responsive, some more jumpy and hard to settle, some forceful, even greedy feeders, some choosy. And while one mother will be delighted by a baby who is vigorous and noisily makes its demands known, another might find the same behaviour not reassuring but off-putting.

THE BABY'S ESSENTIAL NEEDS

However, although every baby is an individual, there are certain basic needs of infancy, needs that must be adequately met if a baby is to survive. The baby needs food, it needs to be held and to be kept warm, and it needs a great deal of cleaning up. These three needs—feeding, holding and cleaning—have psychological concomitants that are no less vital to the healthy survival of the infant. The child's world must offer something adequate in the way of these three things and then it is in a sense up to each individual baby what he or she makes of the care given.

Feeding

Perhaps we would all put food first on the list of priorities, though it is not sufficient alone. The baby takes in far more than milk at every feed. Not every feed is good but all babies in ordinary circumstances have the experience of a great number of feeds that are, by and large, satisfactory. The baby starts off obscurely but urgently wanting something. The breast or the bottle fits this lack and this is the chance for the baby to feel repeatedly that where there was an emptiness and a wish, there is now understanding of what is needed and a hole is filled. We only have to think how the language of hunger satisfied follows us through life, often referring to our deepest needs. We are thirsty for knowledge, hungry for affection. All through our lives there will be recurring versions of this—a hunger for input, love, attention of a sort which is satisfying. What goes in with the milk is something on the emotional plane. For the baby, this is not only a simple feeling of a need fulfilled, a hungry child who sucks vigorously at the bottle and feels his stomach fill up. The child also needs, at least from time to time, the experience of goodness being projected into him at an emotional level. Naturally no parent will be unwaveringly loving and positive during every feed, but all babies need carers who will from time to time feel with conviction 'What a nice baby! What a lovely baby!'

As babies have experience of satisfying feeds, these tie up with a variety of other experiences to be absorbed and put away in their minds. Just as nourishing feeds go to make up healthy bodies, so nourishing experiences go to make up mind and character. Good and bad experiences alike are taken in and digested.

Holding

The second absolute need for a baby is to be held. I do not mean that a baby needs to be held in somebody's arms all the time, but that he or she cannot be left alone for long. An abandoned baby soon dies. We see how new babies long to be grasped; crying babies are settled by being wrapped up firmly; they burrow their way into the corner of the cot so that their heads can find a place which holds them. For the time being they need some of the shaping qualities they have experienced inside their mothers, and some of our most primitive anxieties relate to a fear of falling, of falling apart and fragmenting. The central experience of being held is that of being held at the mother's breast, which is the prototype for all sorts of infant feeding. There are two aspects observable in this holding; there is the structure that contains, and there is the focal point that organises. The mother's arms support the baby's head and back and her lap sustains the weight. This surrounding solidity gives the baby the experience of being shaped and helps it to know where it begins and ends. Then the nipple is the focus of attention. New babies root for it; they are on the alert for this object, which catches and holds them just as very soon the mother's eye will catch them and focus their gaze.

Throughout our life we continue to need structure and focus. We need plans, time-tables and calendars; we need some sort of predictability that we can learn to hold on to. We need a circle of family and friends and we need jobs to go to. We need something to back us up and give life shape, combined with an aim, a goal and interests. The earliest precursors of this are the experiences of being held, partly at a physical level, and then increasingly at a mental one, as the infant's mind begins to use the aid afforded by repeated experience and routine.

The need for being held goes very deep. An infant needs holding in mind just as much as holding in body. The state of mind of the new mother is one where the baby is hardly out of her mind at all and in good circumstances, of course, this is a preoccupation that she does not carry alone but with the help of other supportive adults. The baby has only just left the mother's body and he or she needs a similar space in her mentality, a space that will gradually be vacated as the weeks progress. Winnicott spoke of 'primary maternal preoccupation' and he means that a new baby needs thinking about pretty well all the time. This is not an optional extra. In order for a baby to develop mentally, he or she must not be forgotten. Being dropped out of his carer's mind—as opposed to taking a back seat for a very short while—is as dangerous to emotional development as being dropped and abandoned is to physical well-being. Most parents do not need to make any effort at all in order to meet this need. A new baby calls out all our powers of concentration. Parents puzzle away frantically at the meaning of a baby's cries. Mothers sleep so lightly that the mere stirring of a baby wakens them. Babies need, for a short few weeks, this degree of attention: they need to be focused upon mentally as well as with the carer's eye. Only being thought about can they successfully learn to think.

Cleaning up

The third of the triad of infantile needs is the need to be cleaned up. We only have to think practically to see what a great deal of mopping up a baby needs and what hard work it is to keep a baby clean and sweet. It is perhaps less obvious to see that for this, too, there is a vital mental parallel. Babies cannot deal with all their own feelings, with upsurges of panic and bewilderment. These are strong words, but not too strong for the baby's situation. Babies are highly intelligent: common observation and scientific research combine to tell us how apt to learn, how quickly developing is the baby's mind. Yet babies are completely lacking in information about the world they are born into. Not only are they ignorant of the outside world; they are also inexperienced in their own feelings. Uprushes of primitive emotion engulf them from within, and these feelings need an adult to absorb and help with understanding them. We all know how distressing it can be to hear a baby crying. The crying conveys unprocessed nameless distress and anxiety, and there has to be somebody there who can (at least some of the time) tolerate that anxiety and not be overwhelmed by it. This process of absorption, which leads to the baby's feeling that a message has been received, that distress has been registered and a problem grasped, often is simultaneous with actual physical care. Physical and mental are only gradually distinguished by the baby for whom the pains of stomach-ache must be felt as dangerous onslaughts by an enemy within, since he has no mechanism for the time being to understand the process he is undergoing. He cannot yet think about his predicament.

Learning to think

The establishment of the thinking process is the most basic and important development in the baby's mind. The earliest weeks of a baby's life are devoted to the establishment of a relationship with a person who will be able to understand the battering (natural and ordinary) delivered by the baby's primitive anxieties. I say 'a relationship' not because I think that there is only room for a relationship with the mother, but because a baby can only relate one to one, in a dyad, and indeed learning to do this is a task in itself. The whole process of not simply being separate after birth, but of *feeling* separate, of experiencing being an autonomous individual, is a long business. A human baby has a prolonged period of dependency. Unlike an animal, a child is dependent for a matter of years and only achieves full independence after adolescence. The first year of life sees the infant start to establish a separate personality. Only by being in close and reliable touch with an adult mind can it start to have a real mind of its own.

The first step to independent thought is taken when the baby starts to be able to summon up the idea of something that is not physically there. Bion calls this something 'the absent object' and it is to his psychoanalytic researches that we owe much of our knowledge about the earliest development and most primitive reaches of the mind. There is a lot of emotional work for a baby to do before he or she can reliably call to mind the mother who is not there. Quite a risk is involved. You have to tolerate the concept, no matter how fleeting, that you are alone, before you can conceive of the other person as not there, as not part of you. With this beginning of a sense of singularity comes the possibility of mental activity and symbolic thought. Being in touch with another person need no longer mean touching them with your body. Mental contact, memory, a space in the mind where things happen, a distinction between mind and body, all start from here.

Thinking for ourselves is the central act of the development of our independent personalities. Each baby develops in parallel a knowledge of the external world, peopled by parents and family, things and events and places, with a knowledge of his or her internal world, a place where thoughts, feelings, memories, dreams and imaginings happen just as certainly as things happen in the outer world. This inner world is a world of both conscious and unconscious events and figures. There is one important distinction that has to be made in early infancy if a baby is going to grow up into a person who has decent mental health. This distinction is the one between good and bad experiences, and it has to be reliable and secure. A baby needs a fundamental sense of what's what, a built-in conviction about what is good and desirable; and conversely, a sense of what is bad and to be avoided. From this earliest and most primitive distinction develops our aesthetic and moral sense, and our underlying lifelong pull towards what is good for us and what is in the deepest sense in our own interests.

To be able to establish this split between good and bad, a baby needs sufficient good experiences, ones that will stand him or her in good stead when bad things happen. If overall resources are rather slender, then trust in the goodness of things is too easily toppled. Every baby sometimes feels this, as does every adult, when a good mood proves insufficiently strong to stand up to the onslaughts of something nasty happening, whether from outside or from feelings within. The baby who has a preponderance of bad experiences is at emotional risk: the bad experiences can come from neglect (being left alone, for instance, to tolerate feelings of hunger and fear too strong for the immature system) or from ill-treatment (being assaulted by dislike) or indeed in some cases from the baby's being simply too sensitive by nature to put up with what another could tolerate. In cases like this the inner resources of trust in a benign world, where on the whole goodness rules, collapses—and collapses not on occasion but consistently and often. The scene is set for the child, to put it simply, to have the potential of growing up suspicious and mistrustful, easily irritated and upset, provoking negative reactions that will confirm his idea that people are innately hostile and the world a hard place.

Those with a solid foundation of good experiences are better based. However, throughout the first year of life there are enormous powers of recuperation in the infant. Just as a baby quickly recovers from a physical illness, it can recover from a state of being mentally unwell if the circumstances surrounding it improve.

Clinical example

It is possible to illustrate some of the points made so far by a case history. The value of early intervention is now increasingly recognised and people are starting to see how far-reaching can be the help given to parents and babies when there are problems in early infancy. A mother and baby were referred to an Under Five's Counselling Service, by a health visitor. They arrived for the first of a series of five 1-hour meetings, after the Health Visitor had set the scene, describing the baby as crying endlessly and the mother as reaching the end of her tether and unable to cope. The following is an abbreviated account of the first two sessions.

Joanne's story

The baby, Joanne, sat thin and tense on the end of her mother's lap, not close and moulded to her body although she was only 2 or 3 months old. Her mother had her at arm's length as she told a story of misfortune and misjudgement. She complained that Joanne cried all night, refused her bottle, was impossible to soothe. When given a chance to tell the story of her own life, Joanne's mother told how she had been left motherless at the age of 12, how she had married young and eagerly wanted a baby, but then how disappointed she had been at her failure with breastfeeding and how frightened when Joanne developed an illness with serious diarrhoea and vomiting. Joanne had been taken into hospital, but her mother, exhausted and unwell, had stayed at home, urged to do so by all sorts of well-meaning people. The baby returned in a few days, her diarrhoea and vomiting better, but in an unsettled state of mind. She started to cry inconsolably, and things went from bad to worse.

The worker listening to this was worried. This mother and baby were failing to connect. The mother was anxious, depressed and obscurely angry: the baby was tense, stiff and wide-eyed, holding herself together rather than being held.

At the next week's appointment, the worker was inwardly very concerned to hear the mother say that things were even worse. Joanne was more difficult and miserable than ever. The worker struggled to think about the things that might be upsetting mother and child, and to offer what piece of understanding she could, as food for thought but with a feeling of hopelessness. Then, as the interview progressed, the mother subsided into tears herself: sobbing she blurted out that she hated Joanne; she didn't know what to do; she was doing her best and Joanne was being horrible to her.

Her mood changed however and she reflected with great pain, 'She's my baby, I love her—I can't bear feeling like this'.

Funnily enough, Joanne herself seemed a little easier in mind. Her mother held her tightly despite what she was saying, and the baby fixed her gaze on the worker in a rather hopeful way. She even smiled.

The worker was left in a quandary. Was this a dangerous situation? Had this case the potential to be one of those tragic ones where a mother attacks a child? She made a decision to alert the Health Visitor and the family doctor, rather than to activate the Social Services, but spent a week of intermittent anxiety wondering whether Joanne and her mother were all right, and heard with deep relief the next week that things had gone much better. Recovery over the next few weeks was rapid.

This much abbreviated account of two sessions can serve to illustrate what can happen when a baby's needs are not met, and the sort of interference in the process of bonding that can easily come about. The over-riding feel of the situation is one of high emotional intensity and this is typical of the earliest weeks and months where—as in this case—a mother identifies profoundly with her baby. In ordinary situations it is possible for a mother, helped in the best circumstances by the baby's father, to hold on to her adult capacity to think and to keep an adult perspective on her baby's panic or pain. Parents need to identify with babies; they need to feel with and for them, but they also need to remain adult. Joanne's mother was over-stretched by the force of her baby's anxiety. This happens to many, but Joanne's mother could not recover her balance.

In this case it is clear that what lay behind this mother's difficulty in receiving, tolerating and surviving the baby's anxiety was the weakness and damage left by the death of her own mother. Instead of going through puberty and adolescence with the experience of a mother in vigorous middle age, able to put up with the demands of a teenage girl, a kind of model of resilience to be internalised, this young woman was left with an unacknowledged but powerful picture of a mother who left her for ever, who was not a survivor. Probably the failure of breast-feeding was crucial. It linked up with Mrs J's doubts as to whether she could look after a baby properly. When Joanne became ill, it stirred up worse anxieties: what was she doing to her baby? When Joanne returned, more unhappy than ever, the baby began to seem like a living reproach to her mother.

From Joanne's point of view, her short life had contained too much difficulty for her immature emotional system to take. The failure of breast-feeding in this particular case seems critical because Mrs J stood in real need of the deep reassurance that this can bring. It brings a concrete measure of a mother's capacity to feed. Mrs J was shaky in this conviction, because of her sad, inevitable, unconscious idea that mothers die on you. Mrs J really thought of herself as nonfunctioning and from this, she began to feel unconsciously that she could not meet a baby's needs, despite vigorous, kindly reassurances which told her that a bottle does fine. Joanne was constantly in the presence of a mother so occupied with her own worries that she was in no position to receive Joanne's. She was full up. Joanne's ordinary baby anxieties were broadcast, but Mrs J was not receiving the message. It is impossible to tell whether Joanne's jumpy and uncontained state of mind contributed to the fact that she succumbed so decisively to the bug that made her ill, but we can be clear that the experience for a baby of pain and upheaval in the digestive system is a very disturbing one. After all, a new baby's whole job is to feed and grow. Joanne had no intellectual equipment developed to understand what was happening when her insides started behaving so unpleasantly and she lacked what is necessary—a grown-up person who is in a mental state to give comfort—to feel confident that bad times will pass. Mrs J was full of panic herself and her young husband simply felt that he did not know what had hit him.

When we think that the experience of illness—hard for a mature person—was succeeded by (for Joanne) the loss of her mother when she was taken into hospital, we can see that the baby must have felt engulfed by bad experiences. Joanne came back redoubling her messages of bewilderment but her cries knocked her mother flat and the feed times started to be the times of mutual difficulty. Instead of smiling at her mother and feeling pleased as the bottle appeared, Joanne behaved in an uncomfortable and unsure way. Her mother felt disliked by the baby. From this was a short step to resentment and hatred of a child who was felt to reject the mother's overtures. Yet Mrs J's fundamental affection and attachment to Joanne remained in intolerable, ambivalent conflict with the negative feelings.

The function of the worker was to absorb some of the anxiety and distress. She received and registered some of Mrs J's feelings; consequently Mrs J felt somewhat better and gradually able to recall her adult status and to look after the baby, partly through finding again a sustaining relationship with Joanne's father. All babies need the presence of an adult mind, or adults' minds, which will not collapse under the onslaught of infantile anxiety. The instance of Joanne is only a heightened instance of what happens all the time: adults are briefly overwhelmed with worry projected from the baby and recover.

THE DEVELOPMENT OF THOUGHT

By the time a baby is about 3 months old, he or she will greet known and loved figures with a glowing smile of recognition. This implies, of course, the existence of memory and thought. The instigation of the thinking process is probably the most important mental event. Babies will not learn to think properly unless they have help: the baby formerly in a Romanian orphanage who has not had what we take for granted as a necessity—one-to-one care from a person who carries the memory of the continuity of his life—will not thrive mentally. His mind will not function reliably as a place where thought happens, despite the emotional discomfort this entails. Thinking means linking things up, drawing conclusions, having ideas, even if the ideas which emerge are unpleasant and unwelcome. Real thinking means pursuing reality rather than believing in magic.

This is hard for babies who are vulnerable, and dependent upon the attention and goodwill of others. The reality of their position is potentially alarming and painful. We can observe babies being flooded with intense feeling—whether positive or negative—as we can later observe small children taken over by fears and hopes. Babies and young children often have to struggle with understanding how things really are, since they tend to believe in the power of imagination or the omnipotence of thought. Fears about what they are afraid will happen or what they wish would happen, often jostle with the reality of facing a new situation.

THE EMOTIONAL IMPLICATIONS OF PHYSICAL DEVELOPMENT

Take, for example, a universal experience—the appearance of a baby's teeth. This is an important event, always recognised as such. From the point of view of a parent, it is a hint that babyhood in its most dependent stage, the stage of the babe in arms and at the breast, is coming to an end. The baby is going to be able to do without sucking, and independent eating will take over. What does it mean from the point of view of the baby? We know from common experience that teething is often accompanied by minor illness, not all of which can be satisfactorily explained by the appearance of teeth. The baby is acquiring something new and (since it knows very well what to do with teeth) must be assumed to be having a range of new impulses which bring new thoughts and feelings. What are these things growing in its mouth? What are these new urges? We could say that the baby is dealing for the first time, though not the last, with a fundamental question: are these things tools, or are they weapons? On the one hand, the urge to bite and chew is in the service of development. The baby longs to reach out to new experiences, to explore things by putting them in his or her mouth, to take advantage of all the new sensations of new food, to be enterprising and energetic. One is reminded again of all the metaphors like 'thirsting for information'. On the other hand, the teeth are undeniably linked with aggressive impulses—with all the range of feelings that connect anger with cruelty, revenge and greed. Biting the breast is the first opportunity a baby has for inflicting physical pain. It is not surprising that the teething baby is prey to disturbance.

RELATIONSHIP BETWEEN THE MIND AND THE OUTER WORLD

The interplay between the external world and the internal continue to develop. The internal world of the baby is becoming more and more of a real place, real in a different sense from the outer world of people and events and things, but with a parallel truth and importance. The internal world is the world of thought (conscious and unconscious), of feelings, imagination and dreams. A place where, at an unconscious level, as well as a conscious one, memories are stored and a complex internal theatre of characters, good and bad, are coming to life.

Babies are constantly observed being taken over by experiences from within. Sometimes these are negative ones—the baby who sees in the gaze of a stranger a frightening reflection of his imaginary fears and who bursts into sobs—and sometimes positive, as with an 8-month-old girl who was regularly heard in the early morning laughing out loud and babbling to herself alone in her cot, clearly fighting loneliness with a powerful illusion of company.

SEPARATION AND LOSS

However, a fundamental aspect of reality must be constantly and increasingly reckoned with. The baby is, and has been from birth, a separate person, and by the end of the first year must make substantial progress in feeling like a separate person if he or she is to prosper mentally. This is not an easy job. Indeed, there are babies (and they subsequently grow into people) who resist this knowledge and cling to a fantasy that they are not alone and experience severe difficulties when proof of separation threatens, with its notion of loss, with the need to utter the word 'good-bye'.

The baby needs practice in being alone, in managing its own feelings and anxieties, right from the start, in small and manageable doses. People would all like their babies to be happy but the truth is that babies are born to the human condition, and life is a mixture of good and bad. Sometimes the best we can do is to keep babies company when they are miserable. Then they have the chance to take in, to assimilate and make part of themselves the helpful figures who will then be there in the world of their memory and of their unconscious minds when anxiety threatens. Anxiety does threaten with all the crucial signs of increased separation that take place in the second half of the first year. Pleasure in independence and achievement is very obvious in parents and children as the baby learns to sit up alone, to crawl away, to consider standing up, to hold and eat a piece of food alone. However, all this is leading to the climax epitomised by weaning, the crisis around the end of the first year, often surrounded by a flurry of anxieties about sleeping, eating and separation. Basically, the crisis is about saying goodbye to the life of the sucking infant. Physiologically speaking, it is now possible for the mother to give birth to another baby. The 1-year-old can live very well without breast or bottle. It is time for the baby to direct its gaze outward, to the world beyond the one-to-one relationships of the first year, and to take the mental plunge into a world where the concept of three people—the eternal triangle—exists.

WEANING

If a baby is actually weaned from the breast or the bottle in the second half of the first year, the goodbye to the life of the baby at the breast is dramatised. But even if a baby has given the breast up earlier or continues to suckle until later, there are psychological events of great importance which take place at this time. A baby begins to get the idea that he or she is a separate person. This is an idea that carries some risks. If one is a separate person, one runs the risk of feeling lonely, of feeling left out while others get together, or of being left on one's own with fears, hopes and wishes. However, in order to develop fully, everyone has to taste these less comfortable emotions. Babies can be observed at this time of life looking quite depressed.

Observation of example (a)

George was observed at the age of 11 months by a regular visitor to the family. His last breast-feed had recently come and gone. He was sitting on the kitchen floor when she came in. He looked sad and lonely, and did not smile. His nose was running but his mother said he was not really ill.

He was rather listlessly extracting spoons and forks from the open dishwasher. He fingered them one by one, dropped them, tried them in his mouth, gave up. Finally he turned aside, picked up a cold damp face flannel which was by him and handed it without smiling to the observer.

We can see here a baby who looks slightly lost and miserable, who cannot find something cheering or satisfying to fill his mouth, whose mood is perhaps typified by the wet cloth he offers to the adult. Does he feel he needs mopping up? Is he at the same time saying something about how he feels?

Observation of example (b)

Six weeks later, George was found in more or less the same position, sitting on the ground but outside in the garden with a shallow bowl of water. He looked up at the observer and a large smile broke out over his face. 'Ook! Ook!' he called. 'He's saying "look"', said his mother. George was filling beakers with water and splashing. He chortled with pleasure and crowed.

The observer also felt filled with pleasure at the way George's spirits had recovered. He seemed to have rediscovered a cheerful relation to the observer and a wish to explore new play. And his development, as shown in his words, had taken a leap forward.

It is often true that weaning is a spur to development. In the case of George, he seemed in a preverbal baby way to have felt quite deeply that something had gone and then to have experienced the reassurance of discovering that he could find the same sort of happiness and interest in new, different things. In addition, his sense of independence had increased. The development of language is linked with the unconscious realisation that we are not permanently attached to someone else: there is a gap between people which must be bridged with words.

DIFFICULTIES IN SEPARATION

Many of the young families who come to the Under Five's Counselling Service at the Tavistock Clinic for brief counselling have problems which are related to what can broadly be called weaning. Reference to one such case shows many typical features.

Clinical example

Catherine was 15-months old and refused to be weaned from the breast. She slept in her parents' bed, demanded the breast at frequent intervals and dominated their lives. However, this brought her no joy. She was an anxious toddler, who seemed timid and suspicious, as though she had no confidence that she could manage without being literally in touch with her mother.

To cut a complex story short, it transpired that two factors were at work. First, it became clear that without realising it, Catherine's mother was putting into practice some of her own worst fears about the future of her marriage. Her own father had been distant, partly because he colluded in being edged out of the family circle by her mother. Mrs C was determined that her own husband should be included in everything—hence the sleeping together, the never being apart from Catherine. It was a shock to her to realise that her husband was getting angry and resentful. As he said, 'I think it's time I had my wife back'. Life as a couple needed re-establishing, and not only for the adults' benefit. Catherine was getting nothing from being permitted to act like a little tyrant, monopolising her mother and curtailing her parents' relationship.

The second factor at work was fear of Catherine's anger. Both parents were unwittingly behaving as though to say 'No!' to Catherine would bring about a catastrophe. Yet considerable quantities of anger were building up in the family system. Indeed, it had been a frightening and unprecedented row between mother and father which had pre-cipitated their coming for counselling. Realising that they were both annoyed with Catherine was quite a revelation to these parents. They were also enabled, in an ordinary parental way, to stand firm and tolerate it when Catherine got cross. Over a period of 3-months Catherine was weaned, moved into a separate room and began to speak and play more freely and with enjoyment.

CONCLUSION

Over the first year the infant moves from the entirely dependent position of the newborn. The newborn occupies a specially pro-tected status as the earliest dyadic relationships are established. But by the end of a year a whole different world is opening, both inside the mind and in relation to outside activities. The baby becomes aware of being a person who can stand on his or her own two feet, who has a life of his or her own in a world where other people have lives of their own. Each developmental step, so easy to catalogue in physical terms, has its equivalent in psycho-logical terms, in the life of the mind.

Chapter 4

The toddler and the wider world

Deborah Steiner

Development is a continuous process, each stage being contingent on and influenced by the previous one. In the ordinary course of maturation, if things are to go well, the infant will establish within himself secure figures who will be a source of strength for his developing ego and who will provide inner containment for powerful feelings and anxieties that threaten to overwhelm him. Melanie Klein showed in her work with children that this process begins in the early days of life and that the establishment of this internal world comes about through complex interactions of projection and introjection. In her paper *The mutual influence in the development of the ego and the id* (Klein, 1952/1980b) she wrote:

> By projection, by turning outward libido and aggression, the infant's first object relation comes about . . . and owing to a process of introjection this first object is taken into the self.

She goes on to describe how the first object internalised in this way is the breast; later the mother as a whole person; and as the infant develops so his internal world expands to include the father and other members of the family.

In her seminal paper *Mourning and its relation to manic-depressive states* (Klein, 1940/1981e), she wrote; 'Not until the object is loved *as a whole*, can its loss be felt as a whole'. Later in the paper she puts forward her view of the psychic developments that begin round about the middle of the first year and which are centred around the experience of weaning and the loss of the breast. She believed that in the very early weeks the infant's primitive means of defence against terrifying fears of annihilation and disintegration consisted of a process of splitting the good experiences from the bad. The so-called good breast, representing the source of all good feelings, needed to be kept apart from the bad breast, the source of pain and frustration. At this early stage the infant is only dimly aware that the mother or carer may be the source of both comfort and/or frustration. As development proceeds, the infant can begin to apprehend the mother or carer as a whole person. At this point fears of loss or abandonment arise, as Klein (1940/1981e) wrote:

> In the normal course of events the ego is faced at this point of its development—roughly between four and five months of age—with the necessity to acknowledge psychic reality as well as the external reality to a certain degree. It is thus made to realise that the loved object is at the same time the hated one; and, in addition to this, that the real objects and the imaginary figures, both external and internal, are bound up with each other . . . in the very young child there exist, side by side with its relations to real objects—but on a different plane, as it were, relations to its unreal images, both as excessively good and excessively bad figures, and (that) these two kinds of object-relations intermingle and colour each other to an ever-increasing degree in the course of development. The first important steps in this direction occur when the child comes to know its mother as a whole, real and loved person. It is then that the depressive position comes to the fore. This position is stimulated and reinforced by the 'loss of the loved object' which the baby experiences over and over again when the mother's breast is taken away from it, and this loss reaches its climax during weaning.

The process of weaning ushers in the stage of development we are concerned with in this chapter, which is about separation, loss and mourning; during this stage the infant is also confronted with the need to recognise its own ambivalence towards the loved person.

In his paper *Breakdown and reconstitution of the family circle*, Britton (1983) referred to the external family as 'the matrix for the child's development—the locus in quo of his personal saga'. It would be rare, now, even for a very young infant not to have some of his or her primary care undertaken by fathers, partners, grandparents or child minders. But being part of a family, as Britton goes on to point out, is also 'the source of our satisfactions and dissatisfactions, the origins of our strengths and the hotbed of our neuroses'. 'Satisfactions' would refer to the child's sense of having a secure place within his mother's mind and in the family; 'dissatisfactions' would be related to certain unpalatable facts of life. As the infant emerges from what Rey (1994) termed the 'marsupial space' of the mother, so he becomes more aware of the mother as a separate person and the other relationships existing within his immediate family. Weaning, for example, presents the infant with the disturbing reality that he does not have exclusive possession of the breast and mother. Her presence and care are not provided as a result of his omnipotent infantile demands, but through her independent qualities and her goodwill towards him. This presents the infant with a sense of his own value as the recipient of care. As he develops, anxieties may also arise as feelings of smallness and dependence, or feelings of rivalry and destructive rage surface on realising that his mother is free to give care and attention to others—father, siblings and herself.

In these early years, physiological maturation is closely linked to the child's emotional and cognitive development. Erikson (1950) captures this complex interplay of physical and psychological development when he writes of the emergence of teeth and weaning:

> At this stage, however, not even the kindest environment can save the baby from a traumatic change—one of the severest because the baby is so young and the difficulties encountered are so diffuse. I refer to the general development of impulses and mechanisms of active prehension, the eruption of teeth and the proximity of this process to that of weaning and to the increasing separation from the mother . . .

He goes on:

> It is of course impossible to know what the infant feels, as his teeth 'bore from within'—in the very oral cavity which until then was the main seat of pleasure . . . and what kind of masochistic dilemma results from the fact that the tension and pain caused by the teeth, these inner saboteurs, can be alleviated only by biting harder . . . it is now necessary to learn how to

continue sucking without biting, so that the mother may not withdraw the nipple in pain or anger.

The point Erikson is making is that the baby feels an impulse to bite, arising from physical discomfort in his mouth, but is also now more aware that his biting causes pain and possible anger in his mother. However this is not merely a physical problem; it is closely bound up with how the infant is feeling—if full of frustration and pain he will feel the capacity to bite as a weapon to attack the breast. At moments when he is feeling satisfied, his loving feelings will predominate and the beginnings of guilt and concern towards the breast will help mitigate the hostile impulses.

MILESTONES

Around the end of the first year, physical developments take place at a tremendous rate. At what precise age, and how rapidly, often seems to be a matter of temperament. The parents' temperaments also might come into play here; some parents may be unruffled if their child is slow to walk; others may feel very rivalrous with mothers of more energetic, mobile youngsters. The two major milestones are walking and talking and both have a major impact on the child's psychological development.

Walking

The world becomes a very different place to someone who can get around in it on his own, who can go unaided to another room to fetch another toy, have a look around or just enjoy the experience of walking. Once upright, the baby can see things from a different point of view and his hands are now free to do other things. The natural urge to explore, hitherto confined to his own and his mother's body, or to things that were given to him, can now be given much wider scope. Toddlers at this stage seem to go through a period of elation when they seem terribly pleased with themselves and their new achievements. They often appear impervious to knocks and falls and a surge of almost omnipotent self-assertiveness gives the impression that they believe that the world is their oyster. This manic triumph is a normal part of any achievement or mastery.

Physically the toddler is more in command of his comings and goings and feels more identified with the adult world. Psychologically he is exploring the idea of being more separate from his mother and of being more able to effect that separation. The outward signs of increasing independence are accompanied by an inner sense of greater certainty about himself. This means emotional readjustments not only for the toddler but also for the mother who has to mourn the loss of the exclusive relationship with the newborn and helpless infant, and adapt to her assertive and self-important toddler. Furman (1994), wrote of this in a recent paper called *Early aspects of mothering*. She points out that nowhere else do we make such a narcissistic investment as in our children and with regard to the mother/child relationship she writes:

> As she surrenders her caring activities to her child and pleasurably supports and appreciates his internalisation of them, she transforms her narcissistic investment of her child and his care into object investment, i.e. she loses the child as a part of herself and gains in love of him as a separate person,

and she goes on to speak of

> the necessary flexibility which allows for ongoing shifts in the balance between narcissistic and object investment. This is in keeping with the bodily mother-child unit during pregnancy and nursing, and the extent to which the mother functions for him while his own personality growth proceeds.

The sense of greater freedom and separateness from mother brings the small child up against further anxieties and conflicts. While he feels, and is, less helpless, his increasing awareness also brings him closer to realising what he cannot do; that the world is not his oyster and not under his control as he thought it was. The narcissistic wound of weaning is touched on again as he has to face the fact of his smallness and vulnerability, particularly as he becomes more aware that his mother, still the main focus of his world, is independent of him, with her own interests and desires. The excited pleasure in increasing mobility, together with the acute fears of loss and abandonment, will be evident in some of the characteristic behaviour of children of this age. For example, a young toddler making a sally forth from his mother's knee will run back not only to get reassurance that he can get back to her, but also to be reassured that he can recover a loving mother, not an abandoned and therefore angry one. Another pattern of behaviour seen at this age is of the child running away and not coming back, compelling his mother to run after him. This is often done in the spirit of a game, and when she does run after him he is reassured not only that his mother is attentive to him and will not let him get lost, but also that she is tolerant and accepting of her child's tentative bids for freedom.

One mother remembered her small daughter going through a very tricky phase when she would cry and whine to be picked up, then cry and struggle to be put down—she seemed to want to be able to leave mother but at the same time not sure that she should. This throws up new problems for parents who have to adjust to this new state of affairs—'the necessary flexibility' that Furman spoke of. Versions of the mood swings so characteristic of this age last into adulthood, particularly when major changes in one's life are imminent—moving house, for example, when despite the attractions or necessity for moving, one longs at moments not to go through with it and stay put!

Talking

From the very first day of life, communication is going on between a mother and her baby. The mother does this with her touch, her eyes and her voice. Her physical care of the baby and the way she handles him constitute a psychological experience which the baby introjects as good or bad. Whether it is a good experience or a bad one will be coloured by the baby's own feelings and phantasies at that particular moment. When he is feeling hungry, uncomfortable or frustrated, this will be projected with his cries into the mother and she will then be felt to be persecuting and hostile. When fed and satisfied he will feel loving and these good feelings will contribute to the good experience. In this way the baby communicates to the mother how he is feeling so that she will understand and respond appropriately. Through her care for his physical needs she is expressing her feelings for the infant. Most mothers instinctively talk to their babies as though knowing that the sound of their voice provides part of the 'holding' of the baby. By the end of the first year the baby will have incorporated this experience of a mother who is interested in him and his inner state.

As the baby develops, sounds more complex than mere babblings begin to emerge, more like words copying the words mother says. The ability to do this springs directly from an epistemophilic urge to make contact but also from the experience of hearing his mother talking to him. By 1 year the baby is more able to indicate wants and needs by means of words rather than signals or gestures, but at first the two come together and the words form only part of the total communication. Mothers instinctively, and probably from their own urge to communicate to this other living being, talk clearly and simply to their babies—telling them what they are doing as they prepare the food, or where they are going as they prepare to go out, or what they will do tomorrow as they get the child ready for bed. Hearing the words from the mother in this way accustoms the baby to sounds and words in the context of a good feeling of security and being included. It also adds to the richness of his experience to hear the tones and cadences of the mother's voice; later on he will draw on this experience when making sentences.

Observational example

A child of 18 months, Michael, loved to be taken by his grandmother to stand and watch trains passing on the nearby railway. Before a train had come he would say, half as a question, half as a demand—'more trains are coming here'. He had developed the capacity to remember previous visits and was able to associate seeing the tracks with the trains coming. The tone of his voice was very rich, suggesting his excited impatience and anticipation, as well as his belief that grown-ups could and should make things happen. Saying the words in this way also seemed to help him to endure the waiting, never easy for a small child.

When Bion (1962) spoke of the mother's state of 'reverie' which provides a container in which the small infant's chaotic and fragmented experiences could be processed and made less terrifying, he was also referring to the child's need to seek out and feel contained in this enclosed arena of care. Similarly, at this later stage, the mother's talking and putting words to things and events gives the child a sense of orderliness and continuity in his daily life.

It is a major developmental step when a baby can begin to use words, that is, symbols not actions, to make himself understood. It is a further advance when the 2-year-old can look at a picture of a cup and know it is a representation of a cup, imagine it and think about it without having to have an actual cup in front of him.

Curiosity

One of the most engaging aspects of children of this age is their endless curiosity and wish to explore. In Klein's view the activity of intellectual exploration is equated in unconscious phantasy with penetration into mother's body, felt by the small infant to be the source of all goodness. If, however, the penetration leads to discovery of an object damaged and ravaged by the infant's hatred and greed but not mitigated by feelings of love, then the act of discovery becomes frightening and may be inhibited.

The kind of relationships the child makes at this stage and throughout life are deeply rooted in, and influenced by, the early relationship with mother. For the toddler she is still the focus of his world and, as I have described, her reaction to and feelings about his attempts to strike out on his own will also have a bearing on how he relates to the wider world. If the mother—or father for that matter—subtly convey that they feel threatened or displeased by the child's curiosity and urge to explore, or that separation is not welcomed, he will incorporate a sense that success and achievement are dangerous and have to be curbed. This may present a tension within the relationship, in that the small child's urge to explore more widely now he has the physical mobility to do it is at odds with his wish to please his parents and his need for their love and approval.

However, there are other factors that drive children on to turn towards other relationships. The toddler's burgeoning awareness that mother has interests and concerns of her own, independent of him, deals something of a blow to his infantile omnipotent narcissism. The disappointment and pain of having to face this unwelcome piece of reality will encourage him to find solace in other relationships and activities, and spur him on to explore and widen his experience with others. Other adults and brothers and sisters become important at this stage and, as his world enlarges, his father becomes an increasingly significant figure, both in his own right and as someone who has his own particular relationship with the child's mother.

OEDIPAL CONFLICTS: BEING PART OF THE FAMILY

Klein thought that Oedipal conflicts were present even in the very early weeks of life, and close observations of infants with their mothers have borne this out. By now these conflicts are gathering pace and are coming much to the fore. Although for the toddler in the average family this may be focused on the father, it pervades all other relationships and I will illustrate this with a little boy called Jack aged 2, who came to see me with his mother at the Clinic.

Clinical example

Jack's mother had contacted the clinic because she was concerned about his aggressive behaviour towards other children in the toddler group he attended. She also complained that he would not listen to her or do as he was told. She was a single mother, the father having left when she was pregnant. At the first meeting Ms Harris was sitting in the waiting room with Jack standing close to her knees. He stared fixedly and unsmiling at me when I greeted him and his mother and introduced myself. She suggested to Jack rather tentatively that he might come with us to my room. It fleetingly crossed my mind that he might refuse, but he didn't. When we got into the room she looked round a little uncertainly until I indicated where she could sit. Jack immediately set to, and with much huffing and puffing, dragged a chair very close to his mother, which he then sat on leaning against his mother and throwing a fierce look at me from time to time. Our attention was taken by this and I commented how he seemed to know exactly what he wanted and added lightly that he was making certain I would not come between him and her. She smiled and said that he always liked things to be just so and done in a certain way otherwise he would become very angry. There was no doubt in my mind that Jack was expressing jealousy and anger at the possibility of his mother having a relationship with me and his fear of being left out and forgotten. Soon he became interested in the toys, examining them and arranging things in the doll's house. At one point two of the animals fell behind the cupboard and he became totally engrossed in trying to retrieve them. He looked at his mother from time to time but did not actively seek her help. She finally got the two animals for him but he seemed to get angry and distressed at this and threw one of them back behind the cupboard. Then he became occupied with the locked door of this cupboard, trying to pull it open. He got his mother's keys out of her bag and tried them, then opened one of my drawers and found a key. He accepted my 'no' with only the briefest look at me. It occurred to me that Jack, an only child, might find the idea of two babies intolerable and that his determination to get into the cupboard was expressive of a phantasy of getting inside his mother to see if there were any more babies there.

In the final meeting with Jack and his mother the Oedipal configuration came up again in a different form.

Jack was reported as better—the aggression towards other children had lessened and I noticed that Jack was more inclined to turn to his mother in an ordinary way—for example by climbing onto her lap during the meeting. It seemed that the hostility towards me had lessened as had the fierce possessiveness of his mother. Towards the end of the meeting he became engrossed in attaching a police car to a tractor with a piece of string, enlisting his mother's help to do this. There was still an air of tenseness about this as though a tantrum might erupt if she didn't get it quite right but it seemed to me that Jack could at this moment invent a game to help him work through the pain and anxiety of his intense attachment to his mother and the problems of separating from her. She told me also that she had joined an evening class to learn the guitar which she was enjoying

> but with a smile told me how Jack couldn't bear her to practise. We were able to talk about how the guitar might represent 'a third party' with whom she was 'conversing' as it were and how this stirred up Jack's jealousy and anger at her separateness from him.

From very early on there is a difference in the way an infant behaves towards each parent. The emotions between the infant and mother run very deep and are sometimes very painful. The baby is dependent on his mother in a way that he is not on his father. The experience of a father who leaves in the morning and comes back in the evening allows the baby to learn about separations in the context of a relationship that is less intense. This would also apply, of course, to any other adult who is closely involved with mother and child—say a grandparent or a new partner. While the child feels secure in an environment where the adults are in the main mutually supportive and friendly, there are also mixed feelings. As the infant perceives the parents as a couple their relationship arouses anger and jealousy and impulses to separate them. He may be reluctant to go to bed in the evening, or begin to turn up in the middle of the night; now he is mobile he can make his presence felt in this way. In the daytime his natural wish to join in any conversation that is going on may become insistent and angry as the parents continue to discuss something.

During this phase the different responses of boys and girls to each parent become more marked. For the boy, his father is a much admired figure to copy and identify with. The baby boy, however, is still very much bound up with intensely possessive feelings for his mother, as we saw in Jack earlier, so that father seems to him sometimes like a huge and threatening rival, who will take mother away and be angry with his son when he wants mother to himself. This is the nub of the Oedipus complex, when the boy wishes to have possession of his mother, but now is prey to castration fears from his father. For Freud this is the core complex of all human relationships.

It also applies to the girl who is also intensely involved in her relationship with her mother and is beginning to identify with her. Her wish to have a special and close relationship with her father brings her into conflict with her mother, on whom she still depends. Girls often become cuddly and flirtatious towards their fathers, to the extent of making mother sometimes feel hurt and pushed out. The baby's preference for one parent or the other can be so obvious at times that it may become difficult for parents as their own feelings of rivalry between themselves are stirred up, particularly at times when they are quarrelling or feeling angry with one another.

There is general agreement among modern analysts that Freud understood female development and sexual identity very imperfectly. He believed female sexual development to be based on penis envy—that is on having to come to terms with lacking something. This whole concept is based on the view held by Freud that at this early stage girls have no notion of having a vagina; that this realisation only came at puberty. This is not borne out by observation of small children and in their play, as we shall see later, both girls and boys show the same primitive notions of, and interest in, holes and spaces into which things are put.

For both boy and girl infants the prototype of coitus is the nipple in the mouth, the first erotogenous zone. From this point, the boy has to make a transition from the basically feminine position of taking something in (to his mouth) to the more masculine position of putting something in (to the vagina). His more visible outward signs of being masculine and like father may make this easier for the boy. The difficulties particular to girls which are based on their body image and functions are that the vagina is not so available to view and to stimulation as the penis; she has to wait for the appearance of breasts and menstruation—the obvious signs of her femininity—and for the babies that will confirm the function and potency of her sexual and reproductive organs.

SIBLINGS

The kind of family the infant is born into will, to some extent, have an influence on development, whether from the different personalities of the members of the family if it is a big family, or whether the infant is the first child. Being the first child means having had the specialness of the parents' sole attention, which subsequent children never have. They have to compete from the word go for mother's attention. What a younger child gains is being part of the hustle and bustle of a family with its already existing network of relationships. For such a child the hurly-burly of playgroup or nursery will not be such a shock. How development is affected will vary enormously between individual children and will depend on a variety of factors: age difference, sex, their own temperament. For example, the first child may develop at a fast rate in walking and talking by virtue of the attention he gets, whereas subsequent children may seem slower because there is so much going on to watch and take in. An outgoing and competitive child will be stimulated by the activity around him while a quieter or more timid child may be content to watch from the sidelines for a while, or even may be somewhat intimidated by older siblings.

Jealousy, rivalry and aggression between siblings are natural emotions and are as much a part of living in a family as are love and concern. The intensity of such feelings may again vary from child to child, and how the parents manage such feelings, both between their offspring and between themselves, will have some bearing on how each child develops and learns to cope with the rivalries of the classroom and playground later on.

Observational example

Elizabeth had an older sister, Ann, aged 5 and a brother Charlie aged 6½ who were very close. Elizabeth's birth was anticipated with great excitement and trepidation by Ann and Charlie and they were pleased and relieved when she arrived safe and sound. Both the older children found comfort and companionship in each other, as though being together helped them to cope with feeling left out when their mother was preoccupied with the baby. While the baby was tiny and sleeping most of the time they could comfortably ignore her; the problems began to escalate when she became a toddler and more of a force to be reckoned with.

The difficulties for an older child with an increasingly active sibling is shown in the following example.

William aged 3 had a younger sister Laura aged 14 months. Laura was sitting on the living room floor with William while their mother was preparing tea for a friend who was coming to visit.

William began to play a game with a paper model of a black bat, which he flew round and round in the air. Laura watched this intently and gurgled delightedly. William flew the bat nearer and nearer to Laura until it was hitting her head, making her blink. William then wrapped it round Laura's head, pulling it tightly and covering her eyes. Laura whimpered at first then cried more loudly. William then picked her up saying 'I can pick you up' but then sat her down hard on the floor. At which point mother appeared in response to Laura's cries to see what was going on. You can see that what began as a game developed into something more aggressive on William's part. One could surmise that he sensed someone was coming who would monopolise his mother but who might also pay attention to his sweet, cuddly little sister. When Laura cried William quickly tried to cover his tracks, be more grown-up and lift up Laura but his angry feelings got the better of him and he dumped her. He was struggling, not very successfully, with his anger and jealousy, not only of Laura but towards his mother who was having her friend to tea.

Later on, when his mother was talking to her friend, Laura was pulling herself to a stand by the coffee table. William lay down near her, pulled her back into a sitting position and then pushed her over onto her side. When his mother came again to see what had happened, William said she had banged her head.

William seemed to be jealous and threatened by his sister's increasing skills. Although it appeared he wanted to distract his mother, he needed to do it through the baby, as though he couldn't bear to know about being still quite a baby himself. Temperamentally, these two children were different—William rather a tense, active child, inclined to be bossy, while his sister, perhaps fortunately, was more phlegmatic and easy-going.

TOILET TRAINING

The fact that so many parents get into difficulties in this area and often approach it with some trepidation suggests that there are deep emotional chords being struck here, both for toddlers and parents. As adults we know that situations of acute anxiety or fear can have an effect on bowel and bladder functioning and sometimes in extreme cases, as in battle, cause total loss of control.

The toddler is now striking out on his own—taking the first steps towards separateness and autonomy. One of the first words he is likely to learn is 'no'—essential for him in his efforts to become an individual with a sense of identity and ideas of his own. In order to progress and learn to do things for himself he must resist his parents' wishes to do things for him. This may mean developing in a different way from how his parents anticipated or wanted. Saying no inevitably contains aggression and rejection, which may at times bring him into conflict with his parents and threaten their sense of being in control and having authority. Such issues of control and discipline come into play with toilet training. Before the age of 2 a baby is unlikely to have gained full sphincter control. After this the child may be physically able to control himself but he also has to be emotionally ready and willing to cooperate in the business of becoming clean and dry—that is, more grown-up.

For small infants the contents of their bodies are closely associated with good or bad feelings. A tummy full of warm milk, a mouth with a nipple in it to hang on to and suck, these things give him the good bodily feeling of a mother who is present and caring for him. An empty stomach full of hunger pangs or wind or a full bladder or bowel give him feelings of pain and discomfort, which he instinctively wants to get rid of by expelling them, thus getting back the good feeling. When the baby is having a predominantly good experience, like sucking at the breast, the expelling of faeces or urine or wind are felt to be gifts to the good, gratifying breast. When he is full of hunger, or rage and frustration, his bodily products are felt to be weapons of destruction directed at the bad, withholding breast just as his screams are an expression of terrifying fears which his primitive ego cannot deal with and have to be expelled into his mother.

At around the age of 2, as the baby is struggling to establish his separateness and gaining more control over his body, the bodily products are felt to be his possession, which he can give up or withhold in his own way and in his own good time. He is experimenting with controlling what goes into his mouth, and he can now begin to control what goes out and when. To some extent the baby feels also that he can control mother too—he can please her by putting it into the potty or, if he is feeling angry and defiant, he can use it as a secret weapon against her. Soiling and wetting, however, may have other meanings; at an ordinary level they signify the uncertain nature of the baby's control; they may also be an expression of the baby's ambivalence about growing up and having to leave babyhood behind and with it the special relationship with mother.

Clinical example

An example of a slightly different kind of communication with mother is Matthew, a little boy of 3. He was, his mother explained, soiling his pants in little bits, having been clean and dry for about 5 months. She could give no reason for this or think of any events that might have precipitated it. She said she was quite fastidious herself and this symptom was very distressing to her. Her husband agreed with this with rather a rueful expression, implying that she may be too houseproud and that this caused problems for the family. Matthew did not soil at his playgroup, only at home with her. For much of Matthew's babyhood, however, she had been distracted and preoccupied with the protracted illness and subsequent death of her mother, whom she had cared for, being the only child. On reflection she thought she might have been depressed and her husband agreed with this. In the final session Matthew played a rather interesting game; mother and father were present in this session but not Adam the older child. We were talking about how Matthew might have felt as a baby when his mother was so distracted from him and whether he might have felt unable to get through to her in a significant way. Perhaps his soiling was one way to hold her attention, as she found herself watching him very closely for any signs that he wanted to defecate to pre-empt an accident. Matthew was playing with the doll's house toilet and the tiny baby doll. He stuffed the baby down the toilet, closed the lid and brought it to show his mother. She rather absentmindedly, as we were talking, opened the lid and took the baby out. Matthew took it back, put the baby back in the toilet and, enlisting Dad's help, wrapped it up with sellotape—there was no way this baby was going to get out! Our attention was drawn to this and we thought this could be in a way confirming what we were saying—Matthew's way of joining in the conversation. I also asked if, given Matthew's age, and the fact that his mother had spoken of her regret that she had not had a girl, whether they were thinking of having another baby. They both laughed and father joked about how his wife was terribly broody while he felt rather ambivalent about another child—there had been much discussion and some tension over this issue in recent months. It is difficult to resist the notion that Matthew was expressing both his fear of being dropped if a new baby arrived, and his powerful wishes to put the new baby down the toilet and stop it ever seeing the light of day!

PLAY

Klein saw children's play as equivalent to free association in adults. Attending to a child's play would give some insight into unconscious phantasies and anxieties. The primary function of play is not communication, though it may at this stage be a link between children who are playing. For the small child play is a way of expressing his inner feelings and experiences and is as vital to his development as eating and sleeping. In the second year of life children, through their play, are beginning to learn about the outside world and how to manage it. They are also exploring the nature and extent of their own feelings and resources when they meet the outside world. They do this by manipulating and exploring the possibilities of the toys and of various household objects. Segal, in her book *Dream, phantasy and art*, stresses the importance of the capacity to symbolise in the play of a normal child. She wrote:

> The capacity to play freely depends on the capacity for symbolisation. When the symbolic function is disturbed it may lead to inhibition. In the case of an autistic child the inhibition is almost total. A disturbance of symbolisation can also lead to forms of play which preclude learning by experience and freedom to vary play . . . When the toy is symbolically equated too concretely with the object symbolised, it cannot be used imaginatively.
>
> Segal 1991

She cites two contrasting examples—one of a little boy of 3 whose mother had gone into hospital to have a baby and who set up an elaborate game with animals and policemen and crashes and ambulances coming to the rescue; the other is of a little psychotic girl who could only play with pebbles and this consisted of sucking them, spitting them out or using them as weapons.

By 12 months many children develop an interest in containers and things associated with them, such as lids and doors and handles. They will spend a lot of time putting objects into things and often, more importantly, tipping them out, like Eeyore with his burst balloon and honey jar in the A.A. Milne story. A posting box with shapes will be used in this way long before the child becomes interested in putting the shapes through the right holes. At this stage the child is exploring the idea of space and shapes and what happens when things come together and the texture and properties of different objects. By the second half of the second year, the toddler will be more dextrous and be more interested in putting the shapes through the right holes or in doing simple jigsaws. Completing a task like this gives the child a sense of order, and a feeling of achievement and satisfaction about what he or she can do.

Children's capacity to bear frustration when they cannot do things, and to persevere, varies a great deal. A certain amount of frustration is very important if tenacity and concentration are to develop. Some children will readily show their anger if their attempts to do things for themselves are forestalled.

Observational example

One mother was observed who had a tendency to do this when she was playing with her 13-month-old baby Tessa. A furry rabbit was put on a chair so that only the face was visible to Tessa. She was quick to see the chance of a game and crawled, smiling, towards it, but before she could get to it her mother picked it up and gave it to her, saying 'There, give him a cuddle'. Tessa showed her anger at being beaten to it by grabbing the rabbit, hugging it very hard indeed, then throwing it away. A few moments later, Tessa again showed how very frustrated she was by her mother's over-eagerness. She was sitting by the baby walker, which was full of bricks. After considerable effort, Tessa managed to prize out one of the bricks which she put on the floor. She was about to get out another when her mother took out two or three more bricks and made a tower, at which Tessa flapped her hands and cried very loudly.

One of the most important functions of playing is that it helps the baby cope with all the complicated emotions of his life—love, hate, aggression, anxiety. These emotions, until this point, have been mainly directed towards the breast; now they go towards the mother as a whole person, and towards the family. Learning to master strong and conflictual feelings is an important feature of play at this stage. One of the things Tessa did when she felt angry with her mother was to hug her rabbit very hard and then throw it away violently. She was expressing, towards the rabbit, the troubling feelings about her mother but in a safe way that did not actually hurt her mother or make her angry.

Throwing toys away and getting them back again is the child's way of working through anxieties about separation, loss and abandonment. Freud (1920/1961k) first observed this kind of play in a little boy of 1½ and described it in his paper *Beyond the pleasure principle*. The child invented a game with a cotton reel attached to a piece of string, in which he threw the reel into his curtained cot with a sound o-o-o, which in German resembles a word meaning 'gone'. He would then pull it back into view with a satisfied 'da'—'there'. Freud observed that the child was very attached to his mother, was a good child, and yet never protested when his mother left him for a few hours. Freud was interested in the fact that the child repeated over and over again the aspect of the game, the disappearance of the reel, which represented the most unpleasurable moment for the child, that is, the mother's departure. He came to the conclusion that the child, in so doing, achieved mastery in a situation over which in reality he had no control. There was also another interpretation of this phenomenon, as Freud wrote:

> Throwing away the object so that it was 'gone' might satisfy an impulse of the child's, which was suppressed in his actual life, to revenge himself on his mother for going away from

him. In that case it would have a defiant meaning: 'Alright then, go away! I don't need you. I'm sending you away myself'.

Freud 1920/1961k

Observational example

Another little boy invented a similar game when confronted with his mother's departure.

Peter, a boy of 2, developed the following game when his mother went out leaving him in the care of his grandfather. He first of all went and stood forlornly by the door where his mother had gone out, sucking his thumb. After a few minutes he went to his grandfather, who took him on his knee. Peter found his grandfather's pen in his pocket and 'posted' it through his cupped hands saying 'gone' as it dropped to the floor. He laughed and bounced up and down as he picked it up and did it again. He seemed to be exploring and going over the idea of things being dropped and found, perhaps as he felt dropped when his mother left him.

Winnicott (1964) said that 'anxiety is always a factor in a children's play'. Peter managed his feelings of loss and anxiety about his mother's departure by inventing a game. His play helped him to escape from the impact of a real situation which he found painful and beyond his control. His anxiety acted as a spur to activity, which enabled him to invent a game where he could have some control as well as some fun with another loved and trusted person.

The very young toddler will play with his toys most happily in the presence of his mother or carer. He does not have a concept of being cooperative with another child. Sociable play at this stage of development consists of playing alongside another child, watching each other intently, copying each other sometimes or handing toys to one another.

PLAYGROUPS AND TODDLER GROUPS

This further step in the process of becoming separate and independent is a vital one and should not be underestimated. As has been stressed throughout this lecture, it is significant for the mother as well as for the child. Up till now the main focus of the small child's world has been first of all his mother, and with widening horizons, his father, brothers and sisters and other members of the family. Now he needs to make relationships with other adults and children in the outside world and, for some of the time, he will have to do it on his own. For the child who has older siblings this may be made easier by having an experience of accompanying them, with his mother, to and from school, and of hearing them talking about their friends and teachers. Having a place of his own will give the toddler a sense of pride and achievement in growing up. For an only child, it may be more difficult, although not necessarily so. It depends to some degree on the child's temperament and the extent to which he has been with other children with his mother.

Observational example

Zoe was about 2 when she went to a playgroup for the first time. There was a younger sister of 3 months. Zoe had reacted with considerable jealousy to the birth of her sister and her mother thought some time at a playgroup would help Zoe. She was therefore keen for Zoe to settle down quickly and be happy at the playgroup both for Zoe's sake and so that she—mother—could have a few hours' peace with the baby. Zoe seemed happy and excited at the prospect of going and showed no signs of distress when her mother left her or when she was picked up. Things seemed to be going well. However a 'symptom' appeared that caused increasing concern to the playgroup staff and to Zoe's mother. She took with her, as all the children did, a lunch box with mid-morning snacks and she would not be parted from this box for a moment. She would not put it down, or give it to one of the teachers to look after. She clung to it and this, of course, seriously hampered her ability to take part in any of the activities. In this way Zoe seemed to be indicating that she was trying to 'make a go of it' by not complaining or making a fuss, but that inside she felt unhappy and insecure.

Playgroups are easy-going places and usually flexible about

mothers staying with their child so that individual needs can be accommodated. For the mother of an only child, or a first child going to playgroup, there will be feelings of pride and excitement, even some relief at having some time to herself, but there will also be anxieties about how the child will cope and behave, whether they will be well cared for, whether she can have confidence in their ability to manage. Now she is having to make a very physical move and hand her child over to strangers: she is relinquishing 'her baby' and must mourn the passing of a stage when she was the sole authority and provider in her child's life. From now on she has to make room for a private outside world, from which she will be excluded to an ever-increasing degree. Children in the early months of going to a playgroup or nursery are often eager to tell mother what they have been doing, which child was naughty (never themselves!) and to show her what they have made. As time goes on, however, this may change, particularly when the child goes to school, and questions such as 'how was it today?' will be greeted with infuriatingly noncommittal responses like 'it was alright'.

We know from our own experiences as adults that changes in routine, or environment, however exciting and positive, are always a strain, and this is no less true for toddlers going to playgroup or nursery for the first time. Half a day or a whole day seem a long time for small children to manage on their own and children show their inner feelings in very different ways.

Observational example

A mother reported that her 3-year-old had settled down relatively well at his nursery and, while he was there, joined in the activities and was making friends. However, when his mother picked him up, before going to pick up the older children from school, he would demand immediately and angrily from her a drink and something to eat. He could not, and would not wait, and this became such an issue that he would make everyone's life a misery with his truculence. The mother finally alleviated the problem by going to pick him up with a carton of juice and a biscuit at the ready! The mother understood that it was not simply that he was hungry and thirsty, though this may partly have been the case. It seemed to have something to do with the strain of being without his mother for a long stretch, and finally 'letting go' into her when she met him.

In the relatively relaxed environment of the playgroup or nursery, children learn more about other relationships that are going on, and about their own inner resources in being able to fit in and establish a place for themselves. Gradually they can learn not only about doing things, like drawing and cutting out and making things, but also about playing together, having to take turns and having to share. It is an important staging post, where the experience of being with other children and having to get on with other adult authority figures prepares them for the rough and tumble of the playground and the more rigorous demands of school life.

CONCLUSION

The period in a child's life from 1 to 4 years marks the transition from babyhood to being a young child ready to go to school. The establishment of a secure inner world, derived from the first relationship with the mother, gradually enables the infant to explore the wider external world, and to extend relationships within the family, with other children and adults. The process of separating from mother, started by weaning, highlights the complex interplay between physiological, psychological and cognitive developments. The child during this period makes enormous physical progress which enables him or her to have more control of their own comings and goings. As well as the innate epistemophilic urge to explore, there are psychological factors resulting from the painful anxieties and disappointments of the Oedipal situation which spur the child to make other relationships. The mother's reactions to the child's increasing independence, which will spring from mixed feelings of pleasure, loss, and rejection, also have an impact on the child's curiosity and urge to explore the external world.

Chapter 5

Kings, queens, and factors:
The latency period revisited

Judith Edwards

The latency period, arriving as it does after the struggles of infancy and toddlerhood, and before the reawakening of those struggles in puberty and adolescence, coincides in the developmental pattern with going to school.

MOVING ON FROM INFANCY

The transition is a crucial one, and marks the gradual emergence of the child from the intensity of the drama that has been played out within the family onto the larger stage of school life. I emphasise the idea of gradual emergence rather than abrupt change from one phase of development to the next because, as at any transitional point, there will be residues of infantile life perpetuated. Indeed, these will remain, in a psychodynamic sense, embedded in the personality. The quality of the struggle and resolution that has preceded this stage will lie at the heart of the child's capacity to change, adapt, and expand: to learn and grow in the new environment.

When in *The house at Pooh Corner* (A.A. Milne, 1928) the animals sense that Christopher Robin is going away, they write him a poem.

> 'It's a comforting sort of thing to have' said Christopher Robin, folding up the paper and putting it into his pocket. 'Come on, Pooh!' and he walked off quickly.

Pooh and Christopher Robin go to an enchanted place at the top of the forest.

Suddenly, Christopher Robin began to tell Pooh about some of the things in the world: people called Kings and Queens, and something called Factors, and a place called Europe, and an island in the middle of the sea where no ships came, and how to make a Suction Pump (if you want to) and when Knights were knighted, and what comes from Brazil.

Despite a somewhat dated ring, what I think this excerpt captures is the sense of embarking on something new, the vastness of experience where the royal family of the nursery, mother, father, and child, have begun a narrative together, and this becomes the bedrock on which will be built new learning about history, geography, mathematics, and literature, and new contacts made with teachers and peers.

Then suddenly again, Christopher Robin, who was still looking at the world with his chin in his hands, called out 'Pooh!'
'Yes?' said Pooh.
'When I'm— when— Pooh!'
'Yes, Christopher Robin?'
'I'm not going to do nothing any more.'
'Never again?'
'Well, not so much, they don't let you . . . Pooh', said Christopher Robin earnestly, 'If I—if I'm not quite—' he stopped and tried again, 'Pooh, whatever happens, you will understand, won't you?'
'Understand what?'
'Oh, nothing!' He laughed and jumped to his feet, 'Come on!'
'Where?'
'Anywhere', said Christopher Robin.

Christopher Robin asks Pooh to come up to the enchanted place and think about him, and exhorts Pooh not to forget him. I think what A.A. Milne may be talking about here, albeit at an unconscious level, is the vital process of keeping in touch with infantile parts, in order that real growth may be achieved, instead of pseudo-growth, based on the repudiation of what has gone before.

THINKING ABOUT LATENCY

Traditionally latency is thought to be a time of repression, order and composure; a time when moral ideals are formed. It is often, psychologically speaking, considered to be a rather boring interlude between two far more interesting stages:

> The next stage in the life cycle for children between 6 and 10 is relatively quiet in terms of emotional development and appropriately called the latency period. If care and prevailing love are reasonably good, the child of 6 is comfortable enough with his relationships within the family to be quiet inside himself. He can turn some of his energies to the outside world, which at this stage is represented chiefly by school with its friendships and sharing of interests with his peers. This is probably why most contemporary studies of this age tend to concentrate on primary education ... So in our exploration of the family life cycle we shall move on to children in the age group between 11 and 14.
>
> Pincus and Dare 1978

So much for latency! The 'typical latency' child is thought to be out of touch and concerned with defensive strategies to preserve that state of mind, as the following quotation indicates:

> This period extends from the dissolution of infantile sexuality at the age of 5 or 6 to the onset of puberty, constituting a pause in the evolution of sexuality. This stage sees a decrease in sexual activity, the de-sexualisation of object relations and emotions, particularly the predominance of tenderness over sexual desire and the emergence of such feelings as shame and disgust along with moral and aesthetic aspirations ... it represents an intensification of repression, which brings about an amnesia affecting the earliest years, a transformation of object cathexis into identification with the parents, and a development of sublimation.
>
> Laplanche and Pontalis 1973

In his *Three essays on sexuality*, Freud (1905/1961d) describes the period of latency as one where

the production of sexual excitement is not by any means
stopped but continues and produces a store of energy which
is employed to a great extent for purposes other than sexual:
namely, on the one hand, in contributing sexual components
to social feelings, and on the other hand (through repressive
reaction-forming) in building up the subsequently developed
barriers against sexuality.

Freud relates the latency period to the dissolution of the Oedipus
complex.

The Oedipus complex must collapse because the time has
come for its disintegration, just as the milk teeth fall out when
the permanent teeth begin to grow ... the absence of the
satisfaction hoped for, the continued denial of the desired
baby, must in the end lead the small lover to turn away from
his hopeless longing.

Freud, 1924/1961m

In this account, biological changes are seen as linked with intra-
psychic processes, but Freud seems to be putting the emphasis
firmly on a defensive and disappointed turning away, rather than
a forward trajectory onto a new developmental pathway, a new
stage of cultural achievement as a result of depressive struggle.
This reflects his earlier idea in *Beyond the pleasure principle*
(Freud, 1920/1961k), where he describes his grandson repeatedly
throwing away and retrieving a cotton reel. This he saw as his
grandson's remembering, repeating, and working-through his separation from his mother: what Freud called his 'first cultural
achievement' being a renunciation. A child going to school may
indeed be renouncing her or his parents as sexual partners, but it
is also vital to emphasise the gains thereby achieved. Many later
difficulties with school-refusing children often have as a major
component problems surrounding separation, which were not
resolved satisfactorily at earlier stages. Many of these difficulties
may remain latent in the smaller setting of a primary school, only
to emerge swiftly following or leading up to change to secondary
school, with the increased demands on the child to be independent
and autonomous (Edwards & Daws, 1996).

So the average healthy child has already been gradually moving
away from the family to the outside world, through the playgroup

and the nursery, and some formative experiences lie behind her: the establishment of the first relationships with parents and possibly siblings, the acquisition of language, the capacity for independent movement, and the beginning of the idea of the self as a separate entity in the world. It is the resolution of the Oedipus complex and the acceptance of the parental couple that heralds the desire to make friends, not in a defensive turning away from parents, but based on an impulse to identify with them and to introject their qualities rather than lose them. The child with a secure enough base, to use a term coined by Ainsworth (1982) in her research based on John Bowlby's Attachment Theory, can now leave home for more extensive periods, and can tolerate being in a larger group with one teacher as a representative of the parents. A child who has already had to face the birth of a sibling and struggle with rivalrous feelings both for the sibling and with envy of the parents' intercourse, can better manage the demands of the group, where an individual is required to hold onto anxiety and manage it to a greater degree. It is vital with the birth of a new baby for the first child to have the help of father to move away from exclusive possession of mother.

In their paper *Oedipal anxieties, the birth of the second baby and the role of the observer*, Adamo and Magagna (1997) describe just such a struggle, where 3-year-old Lucia is engaged in a powerful battle to deny reality: 'I am a bit a little mummy, and a bit a little girl'. She uses the observer as a third paternal force to work through her passionate concerns. This struggle, if successfully negotiated, makes a firm foundation so that the next challenge, going to school, is likely to be less daunting.

It is at this point in a child's life that the super-ego (first introduced as a concept by Freud in 1923/1961l in *The ego and the id*), becomes a dominant force, as he or she stops trying to satisfy Oedipal wishes, which have been prohibited, and internalises the prohibition. Kleinian and post-Kleinian thinkers have extended this notion, and Steiner (1996) indicates that a true resolution of the Oedipus complex will come about by the parents' sensitive helping of the child to come to terms with the real situation, rather than by fear of castration: 'In my view, the classical description of the dissolution of the Oedipus complex as a result of castration threats from the father, leads not to a true resolution but to a psychic retreat based on grievance'. The super-ego will, according to Freud, become refined in the light of social and cultural requirements in terms of education, religion, and morality. It is at this stage that a child identifies with the parents' qualities and values, much as the parents were influenced by their early experiences and by the qualities and values of their own parents. Children may become preoccupied with rules and structures as they struggle to take on the new demands made of them in the external world.

A NEW DOOR OPENS

A 20-year-old man, when talking about his first school memories, spoke of the door of the classroom, whose colour he still remembered, and waving goodbye to his mother from the classroom window. This seems very aptly to illustrate the important frontier of school life where the next series of developmental tasks will unfold. In the book *The emotional experience of learning and teaching*, Salzberger-Wittenberg et al. (1983) describe the first day at school for a little girl called Jane. Jane was looking forward to going to school, and on the big day she walked away proudly, with scarcely a backward glance at her mother. The following day, however, she complained that the children were horrible and school was boring. The dinner lady had insisted she finished her food. After the weekend she had a stomach-ache, and begged in tears to stay at home.

As the author points out, although enthusiasm may be appropriate, if a child shows no worry at the separation and the beginning of the new experience, that in itself may be a cause for concern. Subsequent talks with Jane revealed a rosy and idealised picture of school. 'Boring' concealed her disappointment that she had not instantly been able to read and write like her older siblings. Treated tolerantly as 'the baby' at home, she found being one in a crowd of other children, all with their own needs, difficult to bear. Perhaps too, work displayed on the walls of the classroom when she had visited before starting at the school had led her to believe that she would magically attain such skills with no struggle. This first transition is one of the most important and delicate in a child's life (and a sensitive reception class teacher may remain in a child's memory for years afterwards). The teacher's role will be primarily that of helping children become members of a group, and now in many schools, a home-visit prior to the first day will help teachers understand the hopes and fears of an individual child. This partnership with parents, initiated at an early stage, may then be fostered and developed throughout the child's primary school life. Settling the children is the first consideration, before any cognitive and educational development may begin. When I asked a 5-year-old adopted child having great difficulties settling, how many children were in his class, he replied despairingly 'a hundred, I think'. For this child with a profoundly unsettling early history, special attention and care was needed, and once the teacher had been made aware of his particular difficulties, he was able to feel more contained rather than a lost child with 99 rivals.

A NEGOTIATED TRANSITION

In her lively and useful book *Understanding your eight year old*, Lisa Miller (1993) vividly describes a situation where a little girl successfully negotiates the change towards latency in a supportive family, first wanting to supplant and obliterate her baby brother. Then she gradually learns, in identification with her parents, to tolerate him and care for him, albeit projecting her own baby parts onto him, only hopefully to retrieve them at a later stage. I will quote it at some length, because it is such an expressive exposition of this process.

Emily was 3 when Sam was born. A family friend knew them well and saw a lot of them. He went abroad when Sam was about 2 and did not see them again until Emily was 9 and Sam was 5. Of course he expected vast changes to have happened, but the nature of these changes intrigued him.

Before he left, he had watched Emily change from the 'perfect little mother' she wanted to be when Sam was born, to a rather cross, rivalrous little girl who couldn't sustain an imitation of the mother she had started out with. She went through a rough patch when it was clear she was furious with everyone: with her parents for having a baby without consulting her, with Sam for being born and being so adorable, with her mother for being big and being able to have babies, and with her father for preferring to be married to mummy rather than devoting all his attentions to Emily. This was one side. The other side was a real interest in Sam and a real wish to be like her parents and to learn to help with Sam. There was also a genuine affection for the baby, pleasure in his development and delight in the fact that he so clearly admired her. However the atmosphere inclined to be tempestuous. Both parents were often very tired: Sam would wake up to be fed, Emily would have bad dreams. Should they struggle to keep them in their own beds? They felt sorry for Emily, taken aback when their elder charming child showed a different side to her nature, but they were also aware of the need to protect Sam. And frequently, they disagreed. Tiredness softened them up, and, like Emily and Sam, they quarrelled. The family friend, childless himself, was rather astonished at the nature of the passions unleashed.

When he came back he found a different family. Not only Emily but all the family seemed somehow to have moved into calmer waters. Family expeditions, communal interests, seemed more possible . . . Emily had lots of activities: she played the piano and went to Brownies. Sam longed to do similar things. It was noticeable that the relationship between Sam and Emily had changed. It was quieter. Sometimes they played together with great pleasure. On other occasions you could see they had settled for a kind of truce. Emily had identified herself as big sister with a teacherly sort of person: 'Sam, hold my hand! *Never* step off the pavement!' Or 'Oh Sam, that's lovely! What a clever drawing!' and 'Did you know, Sam's learning to read!' Emily, if truth be told, was a bit condescending.

Miller 1993

This lively description of the negotiations needed in the family for development to take place illustrates a cycle of disequilibrium that is resolved, only for new imbalances to occur. Parents, like their children, grow and change throughout the family's development, as they recall their own histories and draw on their previous experiences as children. In responding to their own children, changes in parenting style necessarily follow.

LATENCY AS A BRIDGE

As a child goes through the classroom door, what lies behind is infancy; what lies ahead is puberty, adolescence, and adulthood. At the time of writing this chapter I was reading *The bridge over the Drina* (Andric, 1959), where the history of Bosnia is delineated in a town where a bridge unites opposing sides. It struck me what an apt metaphor this was for the period of latency. The bridge, built over the centuries with a history both murderous and lyrical, spanned the turbulent waters of the river Drina. A walk on the bridge gave the inhabitants new perspectives, different views. In a similar way, if the tasks of infancy have been negotiated in a good enough way, then an area of relative calm is established between the two tracts of experience of infancy and puberty and adolescence. The struggles with sexuality gradually decrease in intensity and are to an extent replaced by struggles with skills, learning, and the development of relationships.

Latency tendencies

A transition to latency which is predominantly successful is essentially to do with balance, so that in order to grow, parts of the self are temporarily split off, but not to an unmanageable degree. In *Sexual states of mind*, Meltzer (1973) talks of the latency child's 'characteristic eye to the future'. A child enters latency with a great craving to develop areas of strength and skill, to work towards being an adult. He describes the hunger for information (Christopher Robin and the Suction Pump) as having its roots in the pregenital conflict, in which what he calls admiration of mummy's tummy riches and daddy's testicular richness fuel further development. There is a hunger for facts (lists of Kings and Queens), which may not yet be translated into insights. This hunger may develop into hoarding and miserliness, and the collecting tendency is at its height during this period. The various branded collections of toys bear witness to the commercial world's catering to the latency child's sometimes obsessive wish to collect and to trade. The bad guys are out there and the messy parts of the self are split off into them, as this humorous class poem given to me by the 8-year-old daughter of a colleague illustrates:

We know Someone who has half a pound of butter on a
cream cracker.
We know Someone who mashes all the food together and
eats it in one gulp. We know a few people who put their
food in their drink.
We know Someone who fizzes their lemonade in their nose
before they drink it: how disgusting!
We also know a hamster that stuffs food in its pouches,
A pig that eats everyone's leftovers,
And a cat that drinks out of the toilet.
We know Someone who stuffed all their food in their mouth,
coughed, and it ALL CAME OUT!'

This composite Someone appears as the repository for all the
messy, greedy, infantile, and anal impulses; and yet in this poem
Someone is humorously acknowledged as being not too far away.

Meltzer (1973) notes the latency child's particular satisfaction
in naming and learning by rote: a mastery based on labelling
rather than enquiry. 'To learn what something is called seems to
them to imply all necessary, or even all possible, knowledge of the
object, act or event . . . as philosophers, they are little Realists, as
psychologists they are Behaviourists.' Again the emphasis is on
collection for display, and more delinquent forms of this include
theft and fraud. Thus, he avers, a poem may be learned without
reference to meaning (as a teacher will describe the child who
'barks at print' without understanding what the words are actually
meaning), and dates of battles learned without thoughts about
human beings being killed. The quest is for greater and greater
mastery: the Holy Grail of 'joined-up writing', and for the status
that accomplishes such mastery. Not until the first stirrings of
puberty will knowledge be sought about life's greater mysteries:
these issues lie largely dormant during latency.

A boy I began seeing during latency, and whose treatment lasted
through puberty to the beginnings of adolescence, told me of an
incident on holiday with family and friends that illustrates very
precisely, I think, that turning point. He and his stepbrother, who
were supposed to be asleep upstairs in their rented cottage, let
themselves into the garden secretly by the side door, and
installed themselves under the open living-room window, so that
they could hear the adults' conversation. What in the telling he
seemed to convey was not only a wish to intrude secretly, to find

out and use in order to triumph over the adults, but also a yearning to understand what seemed mysterious: the relationships between the grown-ups, what it meant to the children now, and what it would mean as they matured towards adulthood themselves.

Sublimation

The theory of sublimation suggests that latency experiences are never in fact free of sexual and pregenital influences. In *From normality to pathology in childhood*, Anna Freud (1980) emphasises the importance of transferring the libido from parents to community in order that the child may be fully integrated into group life. As she points out, disturbances in adaptation to the group can be directly linked with some delay in the working-through of the relationship with the parents. The latency child, therefore, relates to the teacher by reason not of sex but of qualities. She talks of a contempt for females being seen as 'the hallmark of the latency boy': he has of course not only had to relinquish his mother as a sexual partner but also as an object for identification; he cannot marry her nor be like her. The choice of playmates at this stage is thus based on identification rather than object love. Anyone who glances into a primary school playground on the average day may see that there develops for the most part at this age quite a rigid separation between girls' and boys' groups, with the need for identification at its core.

Whereas Freud's notion of sublimation indicated a defensive turning away, where unconscious thoughts are subsequently coloured by fear of retaliation from an angry parent, subsequent thinking has rather changed this original formulation. Sublimation, seen to be at the heart of symbol formation and psychological development, is now considered to be very different from a defensive form of renunciation or diversion of impulses. With help from good-enough parents, a child can embark on the next vital stage of development unhampered by excessive guilt. 'Sublimation will then have dealt with the preservation of the good experience of the cooperative and creative endeavour of the creative couple' (Hering, 1997).

But while this sublimation is taking place, the picture is complicated by the sexual energy still bubbling under the surface. Both Anna Freud (1980) and Klein (1932/1980a) describe the latency child's intense preoccupation with the struggle against masturbation.

After any irruption and satisfaction of the sexual need, a child may well seek punishment, and thus relief, through provocative behaviour. Many child psychotherapists will echo Anna Freud's sentiments about the closing off from infantile experience that can often make therapy with this age group so difficult. For, as she said, 'for the disturbed child the need for therapy does not decrease, but the willingness to undergo it does'. It may take many months when a psychotherapist has to endure the stonewalling and obstinate silence of a latency child's rigid defence, before there develops enough trust in the psychotherapist as an object to bear what lies behind the wall. As with little Jane after her disappointment with school, for whom 'boring' meant a failure of omnipotence, so the word 'boring' can be a coverall for a whole range of painful feelings that may lie below, unavailable both to patient and therapist alike in the early months. It is in such circumstances that the worker relies on a minute monitoring of counter transference feelings; what she herself is experiencing in this defensive vacuum, to give some clues as to what may lie underneath.

The facilitative split

It is crucial to recognise the *essential* nature of the process of sublimation for learning to take place: powerful splitting and repressive forces can be seen as 'facilitative', as Winnicott (1965) described them. Alvarez (1989) points out that 'concentration on a thought, a task, a subject, requires focusing of attention, but it also requires the capacity to ignore other tasks, thoughts and subjects'. It seems to require the willingness of thoughts, tasks, and subjects to remain in the background, what she describes as 'a certain sort of object relation with one's own thoughts'. As she insists, splitting in this context is by no means defensive, but possesses an important developmental function.

A few years ago I treated a 6-year-old girl where there was a possibility that she had been sexually abused by her father and also the certainty that she had been confused and intruded into on an emotional and psychological level by both parents. She had changed her name in order to split off the abused part, and had retreated into a powerfully infantile and narcissistic state. For this child what was vital was not to inflame an already volatile state by concentrating on the abuse, but to help her gradually towards a latency state, where the appropriate developmental tasks could be tackled without the intrusion of unwanted thoughts. Adequate splitting needs to precede integration. I was delighted when after many months of work, she brought to the sessions a *Junior Fact File*, and began to educate me about the countries of the world, strange facts about animals, and to show me lists of her favourite food, games, colours, girls' names, boys' names . . . Like A.A. Milne's Christopher Robin, she was now able to embark again on a developmental voyage that had been interrupted by adverse external circumstances and their impact on her internal world. Whereas for a healthy latency child understanding may be increased by an interpretation about what may lie underneath, rigidly locked away, for a deprived or borderline child there often needs to be an adequate splitting off in order for the saner parts of the mind to be less overwhelmed (Alvarez, 1992). Of course these thoughts have technical implications for the clinician which lie beyond the scope of this chapter.

PLAYING AND WORKING

Klein (1932/1980a) talked of the difficulty of treating a latency child. These children, she maintained, had neither the insight nor the desire to be cured that an adult hopefully possesses in some measure. They were not so powerfully and directly in touch with conflicts as younger children who 'put these things in front of us straight away'. She talks of the latency child's 'distrust and reserve,' which she sees as being derived from their intense preoccupation with masturbation and a consequent resistance to thinking about anything to do with sexual enquiry. As she says, 'the small child is still under the immediate and powerful influence of its instinctual experiences and phantasies, whereas the latency child has already de-sexualised these experiences and phantasies more completely, and given them another form'. As previously suggested, much thought needs to be given to the question of when to respect an appropriate defence, and when to broach it in the service of bringing some understanding and consequent relief.

Klein also observes that play has become more adapted to reality and is less imaginative than the play of the small child. She describes how water play is diverted from oral and anal wishes to do with swallowing, wetting, and dirtying, and takes on rationalised forms like cooking and cleaning. She talks of this 'obsessional over-emphasis of reality' as being part and parcel of the special developmental conditions of the latency period. The lid is tightly on, covering memories of raw infantile life, and the latency child is characteristically concerned to keep it there. There is a need for certainty, rules and structures, both to keep out earlier doubts and fears and to contain the new ones attendant on the acquisition of new skills and new experiences in a larger context than that of the family. As Anna Freud (1980) pointed out, materials previously used aggressively and destructively become used in a more constructive way, towards the building, planning, sharing, and learning needed in order to adapt to communal life. The ability to play is metamorphosed into the ability to work, with a gradual transition from the instantaneous gratification of the pleasure principle to the deferred gratification of the reality principle: the capacity to wait, to carry out a plan. This gradual transition is reflected in the increasingly structured curriculum offered to primary school children, so that their developmental potential can be harnessed and enhanced.

Sigmund Freud was once asked what he thought a normal person should be able to do well. As Erickson (1950) observed, Freud's succinct reply 'lieben und arbeiten'—'to love and to work' is difficult to improve, though as workers with children we would of course include the ability to play as a vital precursor to these adult capacities. Freud was indicating that there needs to be a balance between the capacity to work and be productive in society and the capacity to be involved in loving adult sexual relationships. The long delay in the physical maturation of a human being affords an opportunity during latency, as I have said, for skills to be learned without excessive interference from libidinal struggles, which are to a large extent sublimated, but which bubble underneath like the river under the bridge. What Erickson (1950) calls 'The Age of Industry' is ushered in:

> a measure of infantile curiosity concerning the doings in the mother's body may reinforce man's eagerness to understand the workings of machines and test tubes [Christopher Robin's Suction Pump again]; or he may eagerly absorb 'the milk of wisdom' where he once derived more tangible fluids from more sensuous containers; or he may collect all kinds of things in all kinds of boxes instead of overloading his colon . . . with

the incoming latency period the normally advanced child forgets or rather sublimates the need to make people by direct attack or to become Mama or Papa in a hurry: he now earns recognition by producing things.

Erickson 1950

(It is this drive that has contributed to the long-running success of such television programmes as 'Blue Peter', where creative thinking around egg boxes and cardboard cylinders prefigures later life designs.)

A latency boy I saw, who had both a low level of concentration and a concomitant lack of self-esteem, was trying to make a paper aeroplane. It was quite a complicated operation, and I wondered how many attempts he would allow himself before hurling the paper away in frustration and defeat. While this aeroplane could be seen on one level as an attempt to escape some severe worries about both school and home, it felt important to me at that moment to leave those thoughts latent. He was about to start at a new school. Eventually after some struggle the aeroplane flew quite well, and I talked about his efforts and his hope to be able to fly free. He stopped, looked at me intently, and said 'Did you have to train a long time to do your job?' I said 'I think you liked what I said just then', and he said 'YES' with heartfelt relief and pleasure. At this point it seemed developmentally important to address the hope for the future and his learning of new skills in order to help this child forward.

As Winnicott (1965) said, 'sanity is essential in the latency phase, and the child who in this phase cannot manage sanity is very ill'. Latency is in this sense an *achievement* rather than a hiatus between two more important stages of growth: it has to be struggled for, cared for, and helped by the environment. Another child I saw, who was a school phobic, told me that he had been watching adult videos at a friend's house, some of which seemed to border on the pornographic. After some time, I felt able to suggest to him that these videos made growing up more problematic, in that they bombarded him with inappropriate imagery and language that falsely coloured his own fantasies and thoughts about growing up. Then we were able to explore beneath the manufactured images to think about his own real anxieties about growing up, and about being in the room with me. As technological advances increase and 'adult' images are made ever-more accessible to young children, it becomes increasingly difficult to offer them a protected time and space, and this needs careful thinking about in terms of the developmental needs that may then be overridden.

WHERE DIFFICULTIES MAY ARISE

Although this book is focusing on the normal developmental processes that occur in the ordinarily good enough world of a healthy child, it is also important to bear in mind situations where for a number of reasons the developmental task of resolving the Oedipus complex is not facilitated by the environment. In her *Narrative of a child analysis*, Klein (1961) describes 10-year-old Richard and his struggles for possession of his mother that prevented his integration with his peers. Richard had two parents, but his father was often ill. In the situation of a child who grows up in a single-parent family, particularly one comprising mother and only son, difficulties may arise because there is no father figure to protect mother from the child's intrusion and help him move on. I do not intend to convey, however, that for a child, being in a single-parent family is a pathological state. While there are real and undeniable difficulties for a parent struggling on his or her own, figures for identification and support can be drawn from the extended family or circle of friends, so that the identification processes needed at this stage can be facilitated. What is crucial is for there to be a space inside a parent's mind where the needs of their child or children can be considered, and where the parent's own infantile needs do not compromise this thinking space (Edwards, 1999).

Clinical example

Seven-year-old Steve had already been excluded from two schools because of his aggressive and dangerous behaviour when I saw him with his mother. What emerged in the assessment was the picture of an emotionally deprived mother out of touch with her son's need for authority as well as love, and with no partner to help. When I talked about the difficulty Mum must experience having no partner,

Steve asserted indignantly 'She has got a partner, she's got me!' His mother had recently started a new relationship which was promising to go better than others, and Steve was outraged and bitter in the session, calling her sexual names and shouting 'You've got a boy to sex you up!' Here was a child for whom it had not been possible to embark on the classic and appropriate era of latency calm, where learning and expansion can take place.

Many anxieties may be stirred up by starting school, concerning the moving on from infancy. School dinners and the toilets may frequently be the focus of worry, indicating a link with infantile experiences of being cleaned and fed. Children may be experienced by their parents as being tetchy and obstinate, as the strain of 'being good for Mrs Jones' breaks down at home. There may be bad dreams, as the child adjusts further to the boundaries being placed round infantile omnipotence. This picture may be further complicated in a family that is experiencing separation, divorce, remarriage, or bereavement. Issues of race and culture as well as unemployment and poverty will all be factors involved in the way in which a child gradually begins to have an idea of 'society', while society in terms of peer group and teachers will begin to have an idea of the child as he or she develops into this new wider world beyond the family. There is now available much thought-provoking research about the way in which the twin issues of identification and identity develop (Schaffer, 1996). Central to the process of helping a child with these transitional anxieties when starting school will be the parents' own memories, and their relationship to their own infantile selves. Steve's mother had little early experience retained in her mind as positive, and so struggled to offer as a mother what she still unconsciously felt had not been available to her.

LATENCY IN THE LIFE CYCLE

While I have until now been thinking about latency as an important developmental stage rather than a hindrance or at best a cul de sac, I want to conclude by thinking about latency states of mind present throughout life. These are states which are never fully outgrown but which may be reverted to in times of stress, or which may remain unmetamorphosed as a defence against more pervasive feelings of uncertainty and upheaval. As Meltzer (1973) says in *Sexual states of mind*, 'we may meet latency in a 50-year-old'. In these terms latency may be seen as a metapsychological description of part of the organisation of the personality. In a chapter called 'Permanent revolution of the generations', Meltzer postulates that the political population of a society could, from the point of view of internal psychic reality, be divided into three groups within two distinct generations, roughly from 18–50 and 50–80. The point he makes is that states of mind appropriate at one developmental stage may make for inappropriate and complicated adaptations if perpetuated as a dominant mode at a later stage. For instance he relates rebelliousness to states of mind ascendant at the height of struggles with the Oedipus complex and the incest barrier. It is an infantile state reworked in adolescence, but can as he describes it become 'dangerously antisocial' by 25. The boy who made the paper aeroplane gradually came to this realisation: 'I can't be nicking scooters when I'm 60', he said.

From our previous considerations about latency states, I think it does not represent too much of a leap to associate them with extreme conservatism. Meltzer's (1973) reflections on this are powerful and stand best on their own, rather than being paraphrased:

> Conservatism is the state of mind resulting from regression to latency mechanisms in the face of adult responsibility and the depressive task of working through the Oedipus complex and accepting commitment to introjective identification with a combined parental object. Its longing for stability at any price inclines it to sacrifice growth and development, just as it sacrifices sexual passion to comfort, being the product of introjective and/or projective identification with separated and de-sexualised objects. It is envious of youth, prone to equate age automatically with experience and therefore with wisdom. The belief in omnipotent control and balancing techniques inclines it to bargaining and compromise, while impaired symbol formation and constricted imagination render it at once materialistic, acquisitive and prone to confuse social roles with whole people. Its respect for titles and offices is therefore automatic, subject only to 'checks and balances'. Being unable

to distinguish novelty from originality, it leans heavily on tradition to save it from confusion of values. Its denial of psychic reality impels it to see all events as 'cause and effect', while even simple cyclic problems such as 'chicken and egg' are viewed as mischievous word-twisting. It disbelieves the history of its own rebelliousness, for it has disavowed that identity and its unique development.

Here we have the psychic structure of the latency child writ large, and what was appropriate as a pause in order for external development to be achieved, becomes a barrier formed to repudiate struggle, uncertainty, and metamorphosis into psychic adulthood.

THE MOVE TO PUBERTY AND ADOLESCENCE

There exists in all of us a pull to remain in latency states of mind, which can be seen in the individual to fluctuate even as fluctuations in political thought can be seen over time. Copley (1993) talks of latency as being a 'refuge from conflict'. She describes the plight of some young people who may feel at an unconscious level so identified with authoritarian aspects of their internal objects (based both on external reality and also the individual's phantasy) that they remain 'stuck' in latency, convinced that 'growing up' will mean a slide back into exaggerated expressions of infantile sexuality. She demonstrates how in Shakespeare's *Much ado about nothing* both putative lovers, Claudio and Benedick, hover uncertainly between latency and adolescent states, each viewing with some dismay the developments towards which the other is struggling, and she quotes Benedick's ponderings over the changes in Claudio:

> I do much wonder that one man, seeing how much another man is a fool when he dedicates his behaviour to love, will, after he has laughed at such shallow follies in others, become the argument of his own scorn by falling in love: and such a man is Claudio.

Benedick is scornful of Claudio's change in musical taste, from the drum to the pipe, of his conversion of interest from armour to doublets, and of an increasingly poetic turn of phrase. Benedick says:

May I soon be converted and see with these eyes? I cannot tell; I think not. One woman is fair; and I am well. Another is wise; yet I am well. Another virtuous; yet I am well. But till all graces be in one woman, one woman shall not come into my grace!

As we know, both characters finally, through adversity, make the transition.

It is a delicate and gradual change when it occurs developmentally, and was put to me movingly and lucidly by the latency boy I mentioned who hid outside the cottage window. After his therapy ended and as he was embarking on adolescence, I saw him once more for a review after 6 months, at his request.

Clinical example

He arrived in a state of uncertainty and ambivalence. It felt strange to be back: which of the children in the waiting room had taken his place? Even the waiting room itself had changed, although we met in his accustomed room. He felt he might never be able to say goodbye, so much was he in the grip of these powerful feelings. Gradually he calmed down, and after a while he told me about an incident that had happened on his way to the clinic that day. Now in his first year at secondary school, he travelled by train. He had been thinking about coming to see me, and had passed on the train the nursery school he had attended many years before. He suddenly remembered how he used as a little boy to stand in the nursery garden looking at the train going by, seeing all the grown-ups on the train and wondering about them, what they did and where they were going. Now he himself was on the train, looking back into the nursery garden, remembering his little boy self, while also travelling on his way to being grown up. It was a powerful insight for him, and a reflection of how he had made contact with different parts of himself, and could remain in touch with them and with his therapist inside his mind. He decided that we did not need another scheduled meeting. He would be in touch if he needed to be: 'perhaps in two or three years'.

I have not had direct contact with him since then, but have heard that he is doing well.

CONCLUSION

In closing this chapter with a description of an ordinary evolution from latency to puberty and adolescence, I want to underline the necessity of the latency phase, its value, and the need for its protection and preservation. Latency is not simply a buttoned-up uptight stage with nothing much to recommend it, a stage to be lived through in order to reach something more interesting. As adults we need to give children this space to grow and develop, before they hit the turbulence of change that is the norm in adolescence. If the latency skills have not been achieved, how then can adolescents in turmoil hold onto these achievements when faced with internal and external testing? Social and educational policy and the thinking of ordinary parents need to take into account the vital nature of this stage, which we should not allow to be too greatly eroded by pressures to become prematurely 'grown up'.

Chapter 6

'It's just an ordinary pain': Thoughts on joy and heartache in puberty and early adolescence

Monica Lanyado

[handwritten margin note: "adolescence" starts much earlier; What about constitutional grown delay]

The last 2 years of primary school and the first 2 years of secondary school contain an amazing assortment of physical appearances in boys and girls. Whilst some youngsters misleadingly look as if they are 17 and sexually mature, others can almost literally be half their size and still be very much children in all respects. Physically mature 12-year-old girls may have to cope with confusing sexual feelings and experiences for which they privately feel emotionally unready, despite their apparent outward sophistication. Small 14-year-old boys who are late developers suffer agonies wondering if their bodies will ever change into those of men. The sense of being unable to control the body's physical destiny can bring enormous anxiety, frustration, anger, and distress, as acne takes a hold or breasts become too obvious a feature on a shy girl's body. This is the age of puberty, which can be protracted or rapid, during which young adolescents reach sexual maturity.

THE AGE OF PUBERTY

The medical encyclopaedia states that: *[handwritten margin note: outdated definition]*

> The time of puberty is established in girls by the first menstrual period following the first ovulation; in boys there is no such precise moment. For a year or two after puberty the whole body seems to be adjusting itself to the altered system of hormones—not surprisingly, since the whole body chemistry is affected to some extent.
>
> Penguin Medical Encyclopedia: Wingate, 1983

Although the age of physical puberty varies widely among normal children, anxieties of not being 'normal' nevertheless abound. Fears that there is something wrong with a body that seems to be constantly changing, both before and after the most obvious physical signs of puberty arrive, are common.

In terms of emotional development, it is even more difficult to define what comes within the range of being normal. During the age of puberty, it is as if the many aspects of the individual seem to pull in opposite directions, and what has previously felt reasonably settled and comfortable in the ordinary child's inner world and bodily experience of him or herself becomes unruly and conflictual. The body feels out of control in ways that are both exciting because of pride in 'growing up', but also at times distressing when more childlike or infantile feelings are to the fore. The pubertal boy may feel that he is physically and emotionally 'too big' to have the cuddle that he longs for from his Mum or Dad when he is feeling upset. There is a tug towards growing up, and there is often just as strong a tug towards 'growing down' and a return to the safety and security of what can at times be perceived (by the child and parents) as the comparatively uncomplicated, halcyon days of childhood. There is conflict within the child between the need to break away from parents and gradually establish an independent, authentic, and mature personal identity, and the need to be cared for by the parents as he or she has been in the past, with all the security and dependency that this offers. There is conflict as well as uncertainty between parents and child when everything seems to be changing at once—physically, sexually, and emotionally within the child, within the relationship between the child and parents, and socially with the increasingly important peer group.

In addition, parents may find that their child's struggles during puberty and adolescence remind them and revive in them their own pubertal and adolescent conflicts. Although this can be very helpful when it enables parents to remember how exciting, but painful, it can be to be a teenager, it can also at times confuse matters further. Unresolved adolescent issues in the parents (such as those relating to sexuality, or attitudes to authority) can commonly persist well into adult life. This can create situations in which parents feel confused about which 'side' they are on when there are clear boundaries that need to be established for their teenager. In this situation they can lose sight of the fact that *they* are now the parent who has to take parental responsibility, despite the fact that at times they still feel very much an adolescent inside. Despite this conflict, puberty and early adolescence are also times of exciting intellectual and creative growth, tremendous idealism, and discovery. Specific talents and abilities start to emerge—for example in sports, the arts, and in personal qualities that deepen as the child matures. Intellectually, there is a large, some would say almost quantum, leap between the type of academic work children are capable of doing at the top end of primary school and what they are doing by the end of their first year in secondary school. This leap is indicative of the maturation of the ability to think in more abstract terms, which comes at this stage of development. Teenagers and their parents feel justifiable pride in these achievements, which may often come as a surprise to them all.

A further sense of achievement and 'growing up' is also reached as children of this age gradually undertake more and more activities without parental supervision. This growing independence and how it is negotiated in the family may well be the source of many necessary rows, where parental awareness of the need for their child to become independent has to be balanced with their worries about their child's safety. From the child's point of view, the thrust towards independence and identification with the peer group, rather than the family, can stimulate strong omnipotent feelings as the adult world comes within their reach. This can lead to a heady feeling that they can do anything they want and no harm will come to them—a feeling that can at other times stand in stark contrast to their equally strong feelings of impotence, ineffectiveness, and humiliating helplessness, when the realities of the adult world (such as the need for money) inevitably crash in on them. Parents may often be experienced as spoiling teenagers' fun and not wanting them to grow up. Excitement can alternate dramatically with the doldrums and depressions of puberty and adolescence, when all is confusion and nothing seems to make sense any more.

This roller-coaster of feelings is intrinsic to puberty—hence the idea of 'ordinary pain' in the title of this chapter. Essentially, for anyone to genuinely 'grow up' there is no way round this process. It has to be lived through as fully as possible, with all the joy and heartache involved. The individual has to develop from being a dependent child before puberty to the point in early adulthood where he is able to live financially and personally independently, forming new love relationships whilst maintaining loving ties and culturally appropriate relatedness with his family. For many pubertal youngsters and their parents, it can seem as if an uncharted gulf lies between these two points in time. Intrinsic to this process is the new need for the teenager from puberty onwards to integrate full genital sexuality, and sexual relationships and experiences, into his or her internal and external life.

Even where parents have reasonable confidence that they were 'good enough' parents in the past, they need to accept that, for their teenage children, they are likely to be seen as being in the wrong. At the same time, if parents have been able to navigate their way through their own adolescence to a reasonable adult relationship with their parents, they will be able to hold onto the hope that they will eventually be able to achieve a more peaceable relationship with their teenager. The continuing availability of a secure family base and emotional containment and constancy, particularly in crisis, remain very important to teenagers who are trying to spread their wings. As in early childhood, the parent's ability to survive the process may often be the most important issue. During puberty and adolescence, parents are there to be left and to be returned to, to be 'taken for granted' when needed and then discarded again when not needed.

There is, however, an important caveat to this concept of emotional and physical independence as in an increasingly multicultural society, cultural differences need to be borne in mind whenever 'normal' emotional development is discussed. Nowadays, we are much more aware of the need to avoid making Western cultural assumptions about how ordinary families should function. This point needs to be noted, for example, in relation to ideas about age-appropriate independence, because what may be viewed as being an enmeshed, overly dependent multigenerational family in British terms, may be a perfectly ordinary family in Asian terms. Similarly, Western family functioning may be viewed by Asian standards as putting the individual's independence too much before responsibility to the family, in a manner that encourages selfishness and disrespect towards other family members. Physical demonstrativeness also varies greatly between different cultures and can be readily misconstrued, particularly when safe sexual boundaries are being negotiated.

Indeed, when thinking about ordinary developmental processes, it is intriguing to ask whether there *are* any 'universal' emotional leitmotifs that operate independently of historical period, culture, or patterns of parenting and child-rearing. I would suggest that the Oedipus complex could be considered as one of these leitmotifs, and Attachment Theory as another. Whereas Freud first described the Oedipus complex in 1905, and Bowlby laid the foundations of Attachment Theory in the late 1960s and early 1970s (Bowlby, 1969, 1973), their original thinking has continued to stimulate contemporary psychodynamic thought. Both of these theories, which will be described and discussed in relation to their implications at puberty, start from the traditional model of the intact two-parent family but will be extended to discussion of the implications for one-parent families and stepfamilies.

A BRIEF HISTORICAL COMMENT

It is important to note that what is now seen as a distinct developmental phase in the teenage years is a comparatively recent perception. Freud said surprisingly little about puberty and adolescence in the sense that it is thought about today, and it is hard to recognise modern-day adolescent issues as a preoccupation in great literature of the past. The teenage heroines and heroes of Jane Austen and Charles Dickens seem to pass from childhood to adulthood with few of the dreadful awkwardnesses that we now associate with teenagers. '*The secret diary of Adrian Mole aged 13½*' with its highly amusing and memorable descriptions of the agonies of acne, embarrassing parents, crushes, fumbling sex, and youthful idealism is very much an expression of our times (Townsend, 1982).

A literature search within psychoanalytic writings on puberty and adolescence as a developmental phase reveals that until the 1950s very little attention was paid to the subject. Papers and books written in the 1950s and 1960s give the distinct impression that the teenage culture was a new sociological preoccupation which psychoanalysis (and society at large) was trying to understand. Whilst the emotional disturbances of puberty and adolescence were not unfamiliar, the general turbulence of what was a new social phenomenon—a clearly defined teenage group culture—demanded attention. Radio, television, and films helped to bring these issues into focus and to encourage teenagers to perceive themselves as having a clear group identity, which was often in opposition to adults and which had its own issues to deal with, particularly around sexual and personal expression. Pop music and teenage magazines stimulated and voiced the conflicts that teenagers faced whilst parents, sociologists, psychologists, and politicians tried to make some sense of what was going on, as in many respects this was a new phenomena that had not been present in their own teenage years. The idea of the 'generation gap' gained wide acceptance.

During this period, Erikson (1950, 1968) wrote about stages in the development of identity in the teenage years and Anna Freud (1969) and her followers described adolescence as a 'normative crisis' lasting a number of years. Winnicott (1963/1984, 1964, 1968/ 1986) declared the need to create a 'moratorium for youth' because they were engaged (albeit often in a troublesome way) in vital developmental tasks, and generally the importance of the adolescent peer group and group processes were recognised.

A general pattern of significant life relationships was identified in which the teenage peer group plays an important transitional role in helping young people to move out into the world, leaving the safety of the parent–child relationships of childhood behind. During this transition, the peer group can provide a major part of a teenager's precarious and rapidly changing identity 'I'm an Oasis fan', 'I only buy Nike trainers', 'Everybody's going to the party', and being part of the 'in-crowd' can feel like a matter of life and death. If you are not a part of an 'in-crowd' you may really not know who you are and where you belong. This state of affairs continues until, in later adolescence, friendships mature onto a deeper level and finding and sustaining deeper sexual relationships take on a vital importance in emotional life. Whereas relationships with parents remain very important even if they are full of conflict, parents have to accept that their teenagers' friendships and love relationships may often have equal or more importance to their child.

In the 1990s, we are surprised if teenagers are not a nuisance some of the time. If they are too accepting of parental guidance, there can be a fear that they are finding it hard to separate and become independent. If there is little evidence of a curiosity in sex and sexual experimentation, there can be a fear of sexual inhibition. In Western society there now seems to be a general acceptance that the teenage years are painful but formative years, ushered in by the physical changes of puberty and all their implications.

PHYSICAL AND SEXUAL TRANSITIONS
Pubertal changes in girls

The changes in hormonal levels that are the hallmark of puberty can feel rather awe-inspiring and frighteningly out of control for many young people and their parents. By the time that hormonal changes have settled, the girl will have developed a woman's body not only in height and curves, but more specifically by growing breasts, body hair, and, most significantly, by achieving the ability to bear babies. If these changes happen rapidly, they can be a profoundly disorienting experience for an 11-year-old girl whose emotional adaptation cannot keep up with the speed of physical changes and the ways in which the people around her respond to her. This sexual development may be widely commented on within the family and amongst friends, and suddenly boys and men look at pubescent girls in a very different way. Whilst sexual attractiveness can be a powerful social acquisition in itself, for many pubertal girls there are also agonies of embarrassment over what they perceive as being their ugly or imperfect body. There can be an awful feeling that there is very little that can be done to control the metamorphosis that is taking place in the body, that the body is taking its own course and the girl has no choice about how she will look—too small, too tall, too big a nose, fat thighs, and so on. Dieting becomes attractive because it provides a way of feeling somewhat in charge of body shape—and nowadays there is great public awareness of the dangers of pubertal girls getting locked into eating difficulties at this time.

Menstruation can be a time of discomfort and moodiness, playing a significant role in a teenage girl's life. The regularity of periods can take a while to settle and there can be the embarrassment and dread of a period starting when the girl is unprepared for it, which feeds into a girl's sense of her body being out of control. As it is common for girls to feel somewhat unwell around the time of their period, there can be a feeling of unfairness that girls have to suffer all this and boys do not. The fact that the girl's body can now bear real babies—the babies that she may have fantasised about when she played with her dolls way back in

Pretty gross and simplistic description

So dated

childhood requires an enormous emotional and maturational step. If the girl is experimenting sexually, despite the great improvements that have taken place in sex education, there can be alarming misconceptions and ignorance about how babies are made.

Although explicit sexual fantasy is probably not quite as rampant as in boys at this stage, it is nevertheless powerful and tends to be expressed through romantic fantasy as well as crushes on pop stars, older boys at school and in daydreaming about the latest boyfriend or person that they 'fancy'. Sexual feelings may well lead to masturbation, but possibly not to orgasm. Magazines for teenage girls often offer graphic information about all forms of sexual behaviour, heterosexual as well as homosexual. The current generation of teenagers appears to be much better informed and more able to talk about sexuality in general and there is greater tolerance in the acceptance of different forms of sexual expression. This does not mean, however, that those pubertal youngsters who are attracted to the same sex, or both sexes, are no longer troubled by their sexual persuasions. Confusion over sexual identity can lie behind many of the emotional disturbances of puberty and adolescence, despite the fact that being gay does not carry the stigma that it did, even 10 years ago.

At puberty, biological destiny asserts itself so that whatever sex an individual wants to be, or feels himself or herself to be inside, the body becomes very clearly male or female. Girls who have been ambivalent about their bodies, wanting to deny in some measure the differences between themselves and boys, are forced to accept how major the biological differences are. For example, school sports competitions in certain areas become more clearly divided into male or female teams. Again a sense of unfairness can be expressed, as boys seem to have escaped not only the nuisance value, at the very least, of menstruation, but they can also have the apparent freedom of sexual maturity and experimentation without the direct possible repercussions of pregnancy, childbirth, and parenthood.

Pubertal changes in boys

Of course it is not as simple as that from the boy's point of view and whilst the physical differences at puberty become so apparent, changing sexual stereotypes as well as the current worries about

AIDS and the need for contraception encourage boys in the 1990s to become more mindful of sexual responsibilities. Meanwhile, boys have a different set of embarrassments and worries when their hormones get into action. For them, there may be the extraordinary business of the rapid physical growth that takes place at puberty. Feet can become enormous before other parts of the body catch up. Trousers seem to keep shrinking as legs elongate as if made of elastic. When they speak, many boys cannot tell what kind of sound will come out of their mouths—their old familiar voice, or a strange, new, deeper one. Some boys are lucky and their voice just slowly sinks to that of an adult male. Many others find their voice 'breaking' at all the most embarrassing times, often much to the humiliating amusement of all around them. Body hair can be a source of pride and problems—to shave or not to shave? What to do with the pimples in the midst of the fine facial hair? What to do about the powerful smells that emanate from the body? How to cope with the fact that you are taller than your Mum, faster and stronger than your Dad? How to stop blushing over sexual feelings and thoughts, and what to do about unwelcome erections that seem to announce to the world your most private fantasies and thoughts.

Preoccupations over sexual potency and size of penis, or fears that there is something wrong with the penis and testicles, particularly as they change physically during puberty, can add anxiety-driven early sexual experimentation to ordinary, age-appropriate, sexual experimentation. Masturbation can be a guilt-ridden and very secretive activity for many boys, but is also an important outlet for strong sexual fantasies and feelings and the inevitable sexual frustrations of this age. There can be times when boys feel so preoccupied with sexual fantasies that, as one overwrought youngster put it, he felt he was just 'one large hormone'. It has become more socially acceptable to talk about masturbation as a common sexual activity, particularly during puberty and adolescence. During the age of puberty, boys may masturbate before they have the physical capacity to ejaculate. This can lead to the mistaken fear that there is 'something wrong' with their penis or potency, when in fact their bodies simply have not caught up with what they have learnt about in their sex education classes.

As with girls, there can be enormous anxiety around sexual identity and homosexual fantasies and activity. Although for boys and girls this can be part of a phase of ordinary sexual experimentation, there can be great guilt and distress over these feelings, particularly if the boy continues to feel sexually attracted by other boys and does not gradually become excited by girls. In extreme cases, teenagers can become severely depressed and suicidal because they are unable to integrate their sexual feelings into their sense of who they are. However much social attitudes have changed, some youngsters find it impossible to know how to talk to their parents or friends about their sexual feelings because they fear rejection and isolation. In those instances where sexual identity is causing major problems in the young person's life, they may well seek counselling or psychotherapy (Laufer & Laufer, 1984). There are some gender identity clinics that specialise in these problems (Gaffney & Reyes, 1999).

Aggression and sexuality

The hormonal changes of puberty also result in increases in aggressive feelings and behaviour. As with sexual feelings, there are important issues of how to express, control, and channel aggressive feelings without causing harm to others. Particularly in boys, there can be a dangerous cocktail of rapidly increasing physical strength together with a dramatic increase in aggressive feelings, which when combined with the pubertal and adolescent tendency to act before thinking, can lead to what seem to be mindless acts of aggression and violence. The rise and fall of aggressive feelings can feel confusingly similar at times to the rise and fall of sexual feelings, so sex and aggression can easily become confused in a teenager's mind. Both feelings are exciting for them, and aggression can acquire a sexual tinge as well as sex becoming a means of expressing aggression. As it becomes more socially acceptable for women to express aggression, some writers feel that female aggression in puberty and adolescence is rising and aggression is no longer mainly the domain of adolescent boys.

The close link between aggressive and sexual excitement can be disturbing for many youngsters, as can a number of the sexual fantasies they may have which they can fear are 'not normal' because of the aggression that is entwined with the excitement. The perversity of such sexual fantasies may be particularly apparent in dreams, and youngsters may become uncomfortably aware of, for example, sado-masochistic pleasures within their sexual fantasies, experiences, and relationships. Chasseguet-

Smirgel (1985) argues convincingly that everyone has the capacity to become sexually perverse, if they have the life experiences that stimulate the perverse core of the sexual personality. Freud also referred to a universal 'polymorphous perversity' (Freud, 1905). It is not surprising that when full genital sexuality first becomes possible at puberty and hormonal levels are erratic, these dawning awarenesses of adult sexuality and sexual fantasy can include perverse fantasies as well as very ordinary and acceptable fantasies. There is a fluidity in sexual fantasy and experience during the teenage years that can be expressed through quite wild sexual experimentation of many kinds but, in the main, settles down after a few years into the wish to have a loving stable sexual relationship, where fidelity and trust are central. Aggression and sexually promiscuous behaviour are counterbalanced by the love affairs of adolescence, where falling in love and tenderness help to rein-in wilder sexual and aggressive behaviour and fantasy, which would distress the loved partner.

THE OEDIPUS COMPLEX TODAY

The sexual taboos that relate to generational boundaries start to operate at puberty and are set within the fascinating context of the Oedipal triangle of family relationships. Freud's thinking about the Oedipus complex was being formulated roughly 100 years ago, and has proved to be a fruitful source of understanding many of the passions of family life. He developed his thinking from Sophocles' tragedy of Oedipus Rex, which he felt encapsulated the central human dilemmas of how sexuality is expressed within the family.

Essentially the Greek myth describes how Oedipus' parents, the King and Queen of Thebes, wanted to kill him at birth because an oracle foretold that he would kill his father and marry his mother. They gave Oedipus to a servant to kill, but the servant could not do this, and instead abandoned him in a rural area, where he was found and cared for. As a young man, he had a fight with a stranger and killed him. He later wooed and married the Queen of Thebes, unaware that she was his mother. It was not possible to escape destiny and eventually he and his mother realised that the oracle's prophecy had been fulfilled, as unwittingly he had married his mother and killed his father—the stranger. The play finishes with him blinding himself and going into exile. Freud felt that this powerful play, which still deeply moves audiences 2500 years after it was written, described a universal theme. This theme is now understood within psychoanalysis in a much broader way than that originally described by Freud. Although it has been and remains the source of much controversy both within and outside psychoanalysis, it nevertheless continues to provide a rich seam of thought and understanding (Britton, Feldman, & O'Shaugnessy, 1989; Emde, 1994; Ogden, 1989; Pincus & Dare, 1978; Steiner, 1985).

Essentially, Freud saw the Oedipus myth as describing the little boy's only partially unconscious wish, to oust (kill) his father and claim his mother totally (including sexually) for himself. His theory became somewhat confused when it came to the equivalent development for girls (the Electra complex), and there has been much debate over the years about the age at which the Oedipus complex first occurs, how it is resolved in early childhood, and its implications for gender identity and the formation of the super-ego. For example, Klein (1927/1975) believed that the Oedipus complex started much earlier—during the first year of life—and feminists have criticised Freud's male Victorian attitudes towards women. Despite these and many more shortcomings, there is a descriptive resonance between the power of the Oedipus myth and the straightforward observations of toddlers and nursery school boys, who can be very clear that they want to marry mummy, and somehow get rid of daddy.

Whereas Attachment Theory concentrates on a network of two-person relationships, the Oedipal triangle, as it is often referred to, is concerned with the complexities that arise when three people are all in relationships with each other. This immediately introduces issues of rivalry, jealousy, and feelings of rejection when the third member of the triangle feels excluded from the relationship between the other two. This triangle of relationships emerges very early on in life, most obviously when the baby recognises that he or she has to share, usually their mother, with their father and other siblings.

What makes a triangle 'Oedipal' is that the nature of the relationship between two members of the triangle is of a sexual nature—there is not an equilibrium or equity in what goes on in the various relationships of the triangle. In the Oedipus complex of infancy and early childhood, the growing child perceives that there is something mysterious going on between the parents, from which he or she is very clearly excluded. This is present in the sexual frisson that the child may feel is present at times, or the simple fact that mummy and daddy sleep together and, in Western culture, the child sleeps in another room. Many an indignant toddler will demand to know why this is and why at the end of a day when he may, in many ways, rule the roost, he cannot also claim mummy or daddy in bed whilst the other parent sleeps elsewhere.

Freud (1905/1961d) felt that the way in which Oedipal issues were resolved in early childhood was pivotal in establishing the future path of mental health and sexual identity. Certainly many of the emotional issues that the child carries into puberty are clearly Oedipal in nature. In the first instance, the most ordinary way in which the child resolves the rivalries and conflicts of the early Oedipal stage is by accepting (in the case of a boy) that he cannot replace his father in his mother's sexual affections—but that this does not mean that she does not dearly love him as her son, or value him any less because of this. In addition, the little boy, whilst at times being deeply rivalrous with his father, and possibly quite murderous in his thinking towards him, nevertheless at other times really admires his father, and wants to grow up to be like him. This becomes condensed into an acceptance of the importance of having mummy and daddy together to look after him, and an identification with the father that leads to a male sexual identity, involving the postponement of sexual gratification until he has grown up. This is the way the ordinary little boy from an intact family enters latency, and there is a similar story for the little girl.

At puberty, however, the previous balance in the Oedipal triangle is disturbed because of the first physical signs that the child is growing up sexually. The child is no longer ruled out of sexual competitiveness because of his immature physical development. Sexual fantasies and feelings in all their unpredictability start to fly in all directions, including, to many teenagers' horror, conscious curiosity (frequently followed by denial) about parents' sexuality. Whilst in early childhood, parents have enforced the incest taboo by firmly but lovingly rejecting childish sexual passions directed towards them; by the time puberty comes, this taboo has been incorporated into the child's inner world and seems to be in danger of being breached in a multitude of ways.

REINFORCING SEXUAL BOUNDARIES DURING PUBERTY

The taboo on incestuous relationships was discussed by Freud in 1913 in his paper 'The horror of incest' in his book *Totem and taboo* (Freud, 1913/1961h). This book was written after he had formulated his ideas about the Oedipus complex (Freud, 1905/1961d), in which he concluded that the real sexual seductions and abuses of childhood, which he had previously felt to be the cause of adult neurotic illness (Freud, 1898), were in fact fantasies about incestuous relationships and had not really taken place. Freud then needed to understand why there should be such a powerful horror of incestuous fantasies and looked to anthropology for an explanation. He detailed the extreme precautions taken by primitive tribes to prevent incest from taking place, in which there are rules of sexual avoidance that must be rigidly adhered to and that, if broken, could in some cases lead to banishment from the tribe or even death. For example, he describes an East African tribe where '... the girl has to avoid her father between the age of puberty and the time of her marriage. If they meet in the road, she hides until he passes and she may never go and sit with him. This holds until the moment of her betrothal' (Freud, 1913/1961h).

Freud concluded from examples such as these that, as societies developed in complexity, laws of sexual avoidance became unconscious but nevertheless remained imperative. Freud was grappling with his theories of human sexuality 100 years ago, and must be understood in the context of the times in which he lived and how controversial his ideas inevitably were. As a society, we continue to struggle with the implications and complexities of human sexuality. Sexual fantasies can be disturbing as well as exciting. They can be alarmingly vivid and uninhibited in dreams and rapidly forgotten on waking because of the anxieties and fears they can arouse about perverse or incestuous fantasies. Some sexual wishes and activities, whilst bringing sexual satisfaction at the time, may nevertheless arouse deep feelings of shame. The wish to banish or even kill adults who sexually abuse children is, at times, as explicit in our popular culture (as born out by views expressed in the tabloid press) as it was in the primitive tribes to which Freud referred.

In our society, in which sexuality is so much more openly expressed than in Freud's times, there are many confusing messages that we give to children at puberty. Films, advertisements,

WTF?

and magazines ensure a constant stream of sexually promiscuous and exciting images, whilst AIDs education emphasises fidelity, the need to limit the number of sexual encounters, and the dangers of unprotected sex. Many children at puberty have to find a way of coping with the fact that their parents have separated or divorced and are obviously sexually active with new partners. This at a time when the idea of parents having sex at all feels extremely uncomfortable because the mere suggestion arouses the danger of fantasies of parental sexuality, which is so close to the incest taboo boundary. Forming relationships in which it is safe to experiment sexually, amidst this raging confusion, is all part of the intricate puzzle of pubertal and adolescent sexuality.

During the past 20 years, there has been a significant growth in society's awareness of sexual abuse within the family. Whilst initially evidence of incest was met with widespread incredulity, once faced, it is utterly condemned. The ordinary tasks of latency described in the previous chapter are inevitably distorted by the intrusion of incest on the child's inner world. When there is sexual abuse by a parent, the quality of the attachment relationship is likely to be highly ambivalent, because of the need of the young child to be cared for by the adult who is also abusive (Bowlby, 1988). When the child begins to develop at puberty, feared fantasy is realised as a deeply repugnant reality, inflicted on him or her by the very people looked to for care and protection. The world is very likely to feel out of sequence and without any order. Quite apart from the secrecy and coercion that may be involved, there is a deep sense of shame as well as rage with the parent, and the feeling of childhood experience and innocence lost because of premature and inappropriate sexual experience (Furniss, 1991).

These youngsters are understandably terribly disturbed in their inner worlds, personal relationships, and general behaviour. Faced with intolerable internal and external conflicts, some youngsters run away from home and may end up living on the streets, in prostitution, or hooked on drugs, or even commit suicide—a terrible price to be paid for crossing sexual boundaries within the family.

ATTACHMENT, SEPARATION, AND LOSS AT PUBERTY

The other leitmotif that I have suggested as a universal theme during ordinary pubertal development is attachment, separation, and loss, which are studied within the growing body of thought known as Attachment Theory. In a number of ways, there is something very paradoxical about the notion that separation between parents and a child who have been deeply attached to each other throughout the child's formative years needs to happen at all. Particularly when there has been a good enough childhood experience in which development has gone reasonably well, and parents and child are close and loving, it is odd that, nevertheless, all parties usually accept that with the dawn of puberty, the child will eventually have to leave home and hopefully find a sexual love relationship within which he will create his own family. After all, if you love someone as ordinary parents and children love each other before puberty, you do not readily choose to be apart from them. Quite the opposite. One of the major sources of emotional security and mental well-being, starting from birth, is the reliable availability of a mother or father figure. Even well on into the primary school years, children need to feel that they can be close to their parents whenever they need to be, and can react with considerable distress if separated from them for too long. Furthermore, in adult life, people who love each other and are attached to each other do not readily chose to be parted.

Bowlby wrote extensively about what he termed the 'attachment' between mothers and their babies. His original observations and theories have been developed by himself and others into what is now known as Attachment Theory, which studies the impact of attachment, separation, and loss throughout the life cycle (Bowlby, 1979a, 1979b, 1988; Holmes, 1993; Parkes, Stevenson-Hinde, & Marris, 1991). This is a rapidly growing body of clinical and natural observation, theory, and research, which is very helpful in understanding how emotional security develops and why separation and loss of those to whom we are attached is so deeply painful and anxiety provoking.

Bowlby's theory of attachment has an ethological base that emphasises the evolutionary importance of the protection of the young by their parents. If the immature human infant and child is not protected and cared for by his or her main carer, he or she is highly vulnerable, and unable to care adequately for him or herself. The counterpart of this attachment-seeking behaviour in the young is the parents' powerful need to give care and protection to their young. In evolutionary terms, without some force that binds the parent and the infant or child to each other, eventually the human race would die out. It is this bond that Bowlby called an attachment. He saw the capacity to form attachments, which are intimate emotional bonds to particular individuals, as being a basic component of human nature that is present from cradle to grave. In Bowlby's view, whilst initially the function of these attachments is to protect the young from danger, attachments are essential throughout life, providing a source of security, comfort, and support in times of pain or distress. As adults, if we are upset, we are likely to turn to those we are attached to in our personal life for help—spouses, partners, family, and friends. The capacity to continue to form relationships such as these throughout life, in which sometimes one is seeking help and at other times one is giving help, is one of the hallmarks of effective personal relationships and adult mental health.

Although there are several patterns of attachment that have now been delineated, separation from attachment figures during childhood, even when these attachment figures have clearly been inadequate in providing care and protection, almost always (apart from cases of very severe privation) leads to distress and profound feelings of insecurity (Ainsworth, Blehar, Waters, & Wall, 1978). This suggests that there must be an extremely powerful force at work during puberty when separation between parents and their child is so important. Thinking in Bowlby's evolutionary terms, this must be a force that relates to the survival of the species, which is more important at this stage in the life cycle than the protection of the young. This force, which arrives with sexual maturity, must be the need for humankind to reproduce—and as our horror of incest indicates, this is something that is unacceptable within parent–child or brother–sister relationships. In addition, anthropological evidence suggests that apart from some very rare exceptions, the incest taboo is powerfully evident in all cultures.

THE 'BROKEN LOVE AFFAIR' OF CHILDHOOD

Anna Freud (1969) has vividly captured the pain and bewilderment experienced by parents and pubertal children alike, by likening the falling-out that tends to occur between them at this stage to a broken love affair. Previously loving and thoughtful children become monsters of selfishness, who one minute cannot see why their parents, at the drop of a hat, cannot drive them miles across town and country to a party, and a little while later, just as passionately, have to be tucked into bed with a cuddle otherwise they can't sleep. Hours are spent in the bathroom with the door firmly locked for privacy, only to have the pubertal girl emerge in the skimpiest of clothes which her parents feel are so revealing that they forbid her to go out 'dressed like that'.

Brief periods of intimacy may be followed by a backlash of outrageous behaviour calculated to drive parents wild and away from their child. There is a roller-coaster sensation of being close and then being rejected, and in the main it is the parents who are being rejected. There is often a sense of old scores being repayed with a vengeance at this time. For example, the pubertal boy who finally finds himself the same height and stronger than his father, remembering his father's misguided attempts to humiliate him in the past when he was naughty, may go out of his way to humiliate his father in return, through very public rows in which all sorts of private grievances are aired. The pubertal girl who has been her mother's shadow during latency may become very aggressive and argumentative towards her mother, as the only way she can find to force herself to leave her mother and become more independent.

There is often a profound sense of discontinuity, in which it can be hard for parents and child to remember that, not so long ago, they felt in tune with each other and enjoyed being together. It really is like a love affair that is going very wrong. The art of it, from the parents' perspective, is to hold on tight and never forget that despite all the apparent rejection they experience, they are still deeply needed by their pubertal and teenage children. Parents always need to be ready to change and to accept the challenge that their children present to them, in terms of their own past and present inadequacies as parents. They also need to be very clear about what they believe in because the issue of where the bottom line is, and what parents feel is acceptable or unacceptable, is relentlessly put to the test from puberty onwards—although this is always an issue that is important in parenting. Every day brings fresh moves towards independence, together with anxieties in the child as well as the parent as to whether they can meet the challenge. Beneath impassioned pleas and arguments to be allowed to go to an all night party at the age of 13 may be the child's anxiety that he or she will feel lonely or feel 'out of it' at some point during the party, often followed by thinly disguised relief when parents say 'no'.

All of this conflict is a reversal of much that has gone before. Whereas in the past the little boy, for example, did not want his mother to leave him at nursery and worried about where she was and when she would be back, at puberty the mother is being left by the son and feels anxious about where he is, who he is with, and what he is doing. The fact that ordinary youngsters can feel secure and safe enough to explore the world outside their home is largely a factor of their assumption that the parents and home will be there for them to return to when they are ready— which is in turn a result of being securely attached to them. It is because they have come to feel secure enough in themselves and able to take their parents for granted (in many of the ways that are acceptable in younger children, but often infuriating in argumentative and rebellious teenagers) that they feel they can come and go as they please. This process of exploration from a secure base is well illustrated by Ainsworths et al.'s (1978) work with younger children. If they do not feel secure, they are likely to find it more difficult and complex to go their own way.

It is sometimes only when parents are *not* there when needed by their teenagers that their neediness may come to light—and then only if the teenager is not too defended to let the parents know. For example, a 13-year-old boy may wish to hang out with his friends in the neighbourhood all day, and argue fiercely about 'checking-in' to home even at fairly lengthy intervals. If, however, the parents should decide in his absence to go out, and the boy comes home early, he may be indignant and worried about what has happened to them. In fantasy, his parents need to be felt to be sitting at home, always ready to be there for him. For some boys, this sudden neediness for their parents may in turn bring intense feelings of dependency, which can feel alarming at this age. When this happens, the parents may never be allowed to know how upset their son was when they weren't there, and a cycle of misunderstanding and a denial of residual feelings of dependency and relatedness may be set up. This ongoing dependency is often small comfort to parents, but a consolation many hold onto as they accept that their child has to separate and become independent somehow and that the anger, friction, and rejection stirred up between them makes it easier to let go of a loved child who, underneath it all, is as mixed-up and bewildered as they are by all that is happening!

Despite all the aggravation, for parents there is often a profound sense of loss, of having done all they can as a parent for their child—but as parents who are veterans of adolescent children will assure them, the time does come when a mature parent–child relationship establishes itself. The sense of being redundant during children's puberty and adolescence is an illusion—but painful for all that. There is also a profound sense of loss for young teenagers, as the loved parents who have been the emotional centre of their world have to be given up—for all the reasons described above related to the Oedipus conflict, and eventually a mature and adult emotional love found. Only then can it ever feel entirely safe to have parents firmly back in their emotional universe. Many of the 'blues' and periods of loneliness that pubertal children experience relate to the vacuum that appears in their emotional life as they let go of, or propel themselves away from, their parents and family, but do not yet know how fill the gap that this leaves.

A further important aspect of the revisiting of Oedipal conflicts at puberty is that at puberty, it is the parents who are the thwarted lovers. Mothers have to stand by and learn to cope with their jealousy when their previously adoring son starts to adore young and beautiful girls instead of them. Fathers have to restrain themselves from macho rivalry with their daughter's virile and sexually adventurous boyfriends. It can be as hard for parents to acknowledge the sexuality of their teenage children as it is for their children to acknowledge that their parents can also feel sexual. Indeed, during puberty it can be impossible to talk about any kind of sexual matter in the family—although frank discussion may be quite possible with other adults, and with friends and siblings. This is probably a further manifestation of the incest taboo, but one which often becomes more manageable later on in adolescence.

SEPARATION, DIVORCE, AND REMARRIAGE OF PARENTS

Although this lecture has concentrated on models of thinking that assume two-parent families, it is important to extend the implications of what has been said so far about the centrality of Oedipal issues, attachment, separation, and loss to the experience of pubertal youngsters whose parents have separated, divorced, or remarried. This is particularly necessary in the light of statistics which suggest that a significantly high percentage of children grow up in one-parent or stepfamilies. It is not clear how many of these children are pubertal, but what is clear is that there is now a fluidity and complexity in many family constellations that challenges previous assumptions about ordinary two-parent family life. This is a vast subject which requires a great deal of further study and thought. What I offer here are some indicators of how this might be approached.

Part of the successful resolution of the ordinary Oedipus complex is the recognition of the strength and value to the child of experiencing the parents as forming a united, loving, and sexual couple. When life experience demonstrates the opposite of this, that the parents do not love each other any more and are in many instances openly hostile to each other, the child can incorporate an image of a very negative, hating, parental couple (Cancrini, 1998; Lupinacci, 1998). Ogden (1989) interestingly suggests that it is the Oedipal couple in the mother or father's mind that has the most profound effect on the child's Oedipal development. For example, if the separated parent has within his or her mind the awareness of a male–female relationship that is sexually creative as well as caring of children, this internal model will be conveyed to the child by the parent, alongside the external reality of parents who are at war. In other words, the absence of loving parental relationships in the child's external world and all the pain and disillusionment that this can bring, can be counteracted by the parent's continued belief that good adult sexual relationships are nevertheless possible.

It may also be that when there is a 'vacancy' in one of the parental corners of the Oedipal triangle, it can be filled in ways other than with a sexual partner, which nevertheless provide the single parent with what is perceived by the child and the parent (unconsciously as well as consciously) as a creative partner in bringing up the children. The emotional security and containment offered by this partnership can be of vital importance in providing the clear boundaries in all areas of life that the pubertal and adolescent youngster so clearly needs to experience through the way in which he or she is parented. The person who joins the triangle might be a good friend, a new partner, a grandparent or an uncle, or, if they are in therapy, it might be the child or parent's therapist. Although the single parent's relationship with this partner may appropriately not be the sexual relationship of the classical Oedipal parental couple, the fact that together they are able to think constructively and sympathetically about the child, providing differing perspectives on how to tackle issues of appropriate boundaries and freedoms, is of great benefit to the child at all stages of development.

When the parents' relationship irretrievably breaks down, the external three-person Oedipal triangle collapses, for the child, into two separate two-person attachment relationships, one with each parent. This has many painful repercussions for the child. Often children cannot accept that their parents have really split up. However much they are aware of and distressed by the arguments and strife that exist between the parents, having to accept two different households can feel intolerable. This wish to keep the parents together, particularly in the child's most private and unrealistic wishes, could be seen as reflecting the deeply felt need to reinstate the original Oedipal triangle, which feels ripped apart when parents separate. It is only with the passage of considerable time, often years, that the child finds a way to deal with the split loyalties and battles between their parents within their minds and affections. It can take many years for children to reach the stage where, as one pubertal child put it, it was better to keep his parents apart because if he did not 'World War Three' broke out.

The physical separation from the parent the child does not live with, as well as the collapse of the internal Oedipal triangle, heightens the child's awareness of the pain of missing someone that they love. If this happens before or during the pubertal stage, these feelings of loss are very likely to interact with the feelings of loss that they would have experienced anyway in trying to separate from the parental base because of sexual maturity. Freud emphasised that difficulties in the resolution of the Oedipus complex within *stable* families can result in tremendous personal problems throughout life, bringing many children and adults into therapy. This discussion is not intended as an argument that warring parents should stay together for the sake of the children. What I wish to emphasise is that there are particular problems relating to the powerful experiences of loss inherent in parental separation and divorce, which will inevitably put particular strains during puberty on the resolution of the Oedipus complex and attempts to separate from the parents. (For fuller discussions of the implications of parental divorce, see Gorrell-Barnes, Thompson, Daniel, & Burchardt, 1998, and Robinson, 1997.)

To return to the theme of the Oedipus complex as a 'leitmotif', what happens to anxieties about the incest boundary being broken at puberty, when parents no longer love each other? How does the lack of a 'sexual rival', or the arrival of a new sexual rival affect the reworking of the Oedipus complex? Sometimes the attachment and love between parent and child may become particularly intense following the loss of the marital partner, with the child at times taking on a prematurely adult or even parental attitude towards the parent. When sexual maturity arrives this closeness may become particularly worrying because of incest taboos. This can lead to rebelliousness and rejection of the parent, which contrasts painfully with the previous closeness. Another solution might be that the child and parent try to deny the fact that the child is sexually maturing and generally growing up, so that the status quo is not threatened and there is no need for any further painful separations in their lives. In this situation the child may find it enormously difficult to break away from the parent. There are, of course, many other possible scenarios. The important point to note is the problem of how to cope with sexuality within a two-person parent–child relationship that is not held within the dynamic of the external three-person Oedipal triangle.

Where the parent has a new sexual partner, there are often all manner of jealousies and rivalries and, again, many different possible solutions. Whilst there may be great relief that the parent has found a new love relationship who may also be genuinely loved and welcomed by the child, there may also be deep feelings of rejection and inadequacy, because the child may nevertheless feel that his or her love was not sufficient for the parent. Sexual relationships may become overvalued as being of more importance than the parent–child relationship, and the youngster at puberty may engage in desperate attempts to replace what is felt as the

[handwritten marginal notes: "Wouldn't the existance of healthy children of divorced parents prove this wrong? What about ACE spectrum individuals? Queer?"]

impending loss of the parent–child link, with their own new and at times emotionally over-invested sexual relationships.

These are just a few of the many possible repercussions of parental separation on Oedipal relationships and attachment, separation, and loss during puberty and adolescence. In addition to the complications in ordinary developmental processes that these teenagers need to cope with, they may also hold a disillusioned view of adult sexual relationships and their stability. This may make them highly ambivalent about any boyfriend or girlfriend relationship with which they experiment, and in the long run deeply sceptical about the potential security and stability of adult sexual relationships. Alternatively, sexuality may be overvalued in relationships because the child, rightly or wrongly, perceives the parents' search for new sexual partners as being more important than caring for their children.

CONCLUSION

This lecture describes the physical and emotional changes of puberty and emphasises the importance of the dawning of sexual maturity, its impact on personality development, and relationships with parents and the peer group. Two key concepts, the Oedipus complex and Attachment Theory, are discussed in relation to their implications at puberty. It is argued that separation between children and their parents is painful, but a necessary developmental hurdle, and one which can fuel a sense of pride and achievement.

From the 'ordinary pains' of puberty, there may be an accompanying exhilaration of emotional growth, creativity, and the headiness of early romances and sexual exploration. These can combine to give a powerful sense of energy and fun that are also the hallmark of this conflicted and yet very promising stage of life.

Chapter 7

Adolescence: A personal identity in a topsy-turvy world

Charlotte Jarvis

Adolescence is a time of great turmoil, confusion, and uncertainty, but it is through this process that we arrive at adulthood. The purpose of adolescence is the establishment of a personal identity, and in order to achieve this the child has to separate from his or her early object ties to parents and achieve a position outside the family. This separation is achieved gradually: by establishing a position within a peer group followed by more intimate relationships. In mid or late adolescence, choices are made about focusing on areas of achievement, possibly involving a period as a student, or on finding employment that will lead to economic independence. In the latter stages of adolescence, moving out of the parental home to live independently or with peers, and forming intimate sexual relationships, facilitates the move into adulthood.

In learning about and understanding this complex period of development we could consider our own experience of adolescence. For some, this is linked with the experience of working with adolescents or parenting adolescents. For others, the experience of their own adolescence may invest this lecture with a strong desire to get a hold of a structure, which will help them to think about and understand this complex stage of life. Adolescence as a discrete 'stage of life' has been recognised and reinforced relatively recently within Western society. Music, fashion, and a wide range of cultural issues are associated with and identified by adolescents as belonging to 'their' age group.

Psychoanalytic theories about adolescence focus on the internal changes that take place as a personal identity develops. This lecture will explore the development of personality within frameworks such as the family, friendships, and wider social networks, school, and intellectual development. These external frameworks are helpful for examining adolescent development because by noting changes in these spheres, we can make links to the internal processes that are taking place.

Early adolescence starts in association with the bodily changes of puberty, which roughly take place between 11 and 14 years. The menarche for the girl and ejaculation for the boy, while physically marking the onset of puberty, may not be the only indicators of adolescent development.

The 'turmoil' of adolescence is directly observable in some young peoples' inconsistent and fluctuating functioning in relation to their environment. For others the absence of overt turmoil may indicate that the changes which take place during adolescence can take place internally and are not necessarily acted out in the environment (Offer & Offer, 1975).

EMOTIONAL, COGNITIVE, AND INTELLECTUAL DEVELOPMENT

Before examining a more detailed psychoanalytic version of the changes that take place in the internal world of the adolescent, I will explore the emphasis cognitive psychologists place on the role of intellectual development during adolescence; specifically those theories which have considered these developmental phenomena in conjunction with psychoanalytic ideas.

Cognitive psychologists use Piaget's theories to emphasise the role of intellectual development in adolescence. Piaget (1975) used the term 'formal operational thinking' to describe the adolescent's emerging ability to think abstractly. Formal operational thinking represents a dramatic shift from the latency child's viewpoint, which is focused on the outside world of facts based on an egocentric viewpoint, to the ability to think abstractly, which begins and becomes established during adolescence. The formal operational thinker becomes aware of a rapidly expanding world in which his or her own significance is shrinking. New ideas and theories are acquired and the ability to think abstractly means that instead of a world based on their own experience, adolescents are faced with the task of integrating their own experience of the world with that of the world of thoughts and ideas.

The importance of these intellectual developments, and the disruption they produce, are considered by Schave and Schave (1989) in relation to the role of parents in early adolescence. They view the psychic fluctuations evident in early adolescence as a response to the need to accommodate the changes in experience and cognition that are taking place within. The Schaves describe the early adolescent stage as being characterised by extreme egocentricity and selfishness in behaviour, thoughts, and feelings. They suggest that the turmoil brought about by the changes in cognitive development make it difficult for the adolescent to discriminate between their own preoccupations and what others may think of them. This can lead to feeling persecuted by what they feel to be others' attention on them.

Parents have a vital role in assisting their children in negotiating the great developmental leaps during childhood. The experience of the toddler within the family can be viewed as the genesis of the struggles of early adolescents and their families. Like toddlers, adolescents need to deny their parents continued importance in order to develop relationships with the outside world. This process produces intense feelings of ambivalence as they also need parents to be available—assisting them by listening, containing, setting boundaries and limits, and providing a structured family that can be turned to when needed.

Another parallel between early adolescence and the toddler phase is the confrontation with disillusionment: their limited capacities and attainments of development produce feelings of inadequacy and shame. For the adolescent, like the toddler, this can result in intense anger and rage, which may be expressed in tantrums.

A different emphasis is explored by Fonagy and Moran (1991), who examine the relationship between cognitive development and the development of empathy, that is, the emotional maturity to see the world from another person's point of view. This model of emotional development outlines the role of developmental phases and, in terms of adolescence, emphasises the development of the capacity to tolerate conflicting viewpoints or internal representations. This model suggests that cognitive and emotional development can be stunted or interfered with during childhood or adolescence. Failure to develop could be caused by trauma, insufficient environmental support, or defensive denial. This implies that active assistance may be needed for the young person who has difficulty in thinking about and representing their emotional world (Baruch, 1997).

For those of us working with adolescents, these ideas provide some insight into the difficulties and frustration we can feel when attempting to talk and relate to adolescents who appear to be unable or unprepared to talk, think, and understand their own feelings and their impact on others. This may not be due to bloody-mindedness but may have more to do with a failure to develop internal structures that would enable them to express themselves and think about the feelings of others.

This has implications for psychotherapists and counsellors working with young people. Such adolescents will need the help of an active mind that can show an interest in what their feelings might be and how their current symptoms, or recent behaviour, may relate to events, relationships, and experiences in their past and present life. In other words, the therapist's task is to help the young person to construct a mind which could think and make links and tolerate internal conflict instead of feeling trapped in a mindless present.

From this starting point we have a framework for appreciating the changes in the adolescent's cognitive experience of the world and the potential of the adolescent mind. Sadly for many, this potential is never realised but this may not be because of limitations in intelligence. Young people need to have an experience of resolving conflicting feelings and this is primarily obtained through relationships with others, which offer an experience of managing the feelings evoked by conflict. Those who have not had this experience will find it hard to manage internal conflict and make progress in their emotional and intellectual development.

It is often the case that during early and mid adolescence young people find it difficult to sustain therapy or counselling unless they have committed external support. The young people who cause the most worry to adults working with them are often the least capable of sustaining a relationship that could help them. This is difficult for therapists as well as for others working with this age group. This inconsistency is partly related to the natural pattern of early adolescence, which seeks new relationships and then moves on or retreats from close contact with adults. What follows is an illustration from clinical experience.

Clinical example

When Ian, aged 16, requested counselling he came across as bolshy but urgently in need of help. I wrote offering him an appointment which he phoned to cancel. I spoke to him on the phone; he was unsure about whether he wanted a further appointment and asked me what counselling would involve. He told me he was having problems in the local residential unit where he lived and was particularly angry with his key worker, who was interfering. I told him that we could talk about this further next week if he wanted to come to the centre and explained that our meetings would be confidential and that it was up to him whether he wanted to come or not. He agreed that I should keep a time for him and turned up on time the following week.

Ian had been taken into care in his early adolescence because his mother could not control him. He now had limited contact with his mother, who had considerable problems of her own. His father lived in another part of the country and had a new family. Ian's attempts to contact him were not responded to. Ian told me he felt depressed and apathetic and had recently been prone to violent outbursts, particularly in relation to the staff in his unit. He told me he was hoping to find work, having completed a computer training course, but he was finding it difficult to obtain a work placement that might lead to employment. He felt pressured by his residential unit who were suggesting that he should move into their semi-independent unit, but Ian didn't feel ready.

Ian came on time for all his next three appointments and in response to my questions and comments we built up a picture of his unhappy and difficult life, which had culminated in his move into care. In his early adolescence he had became involved with a delinquent gang and this resulted in him being arrested and taken into care. He felt that this had helped him to move away from the gang and vividly explained how much he had enjoyed Outward Bound holidays organised by his children's home. We established that he desperately wanted to have a better life and hoped his training course would lead to economic independence.

In my experience it is vitally important for adolescents to feel that they can become good or expert in various fields, and it is important for adults working with them to recognise and support these hopes and aspirations. This is particularly so for deprived or traumatised adolescents who need this to be thought about, remembered, and balanced against their emotional difficulties and the problems they create (Bloch, 1995).

During my meetings with Ian I took care to balance my acknowledgement of his anger and disappointment about his situation against these aspirations. It became clearer that the changes he was facing were jeopardised by feelings that were rooted in his childhood and the loss of both his parents. In his third meeting with me his anger and disappointment merged with his fear and terror about whether he could manage his future. He began to cry, and as he told me about his loneliness and fear he wept. This 6-foot young man mopped up his tears with a small towel he produced from his pocket. It was one of those towels that mops up beer spills on a bar counter . . . This poignant moment remains with me as a powerful image of the muddle and confusion that some adolescents face; they have to manage the child within them as well as face their future as adults.

During our meetings I helped Ian to think about and understand why this work placement, which was so important to him, was such a difficult transition. He was able to acknowledge that he needed support in order to present himself at interviews and cope with the demands of a regular job. He had an interview lined up after our last meeting and did not return to see me again.

To have such an intense contact ended in this way can be unsettling and disappointing for the therapist. He left me feeling concerned about him and unsure about whether I had helped enough. More than anything I felt dropped. Ian needed to work through his extremely painful grief in a supportive and confidential setting. The way he ended our contact meant that I was faced with the task of managing difficult feelings about transition, rejection, and disappointment. Most adolescents create feelings of inadequacy and anxiety in the adults who care about them; Ian left these feelings with me and I hope that, having done this, he was able to move on in his development. In the future, he may turn again to therapy when he finds that he is struggling.

My contact with Ian also draws attention to the complex process adolescents have to negotiate as they move into the world of work and assume more responsibility for themselves. His difficulties illustrate how the natural conclusion of adolescent development is dependent on both external circumstances and the adolescent's internal resources. These factors are explored in 'Leaving Home,' later in this lecture.

PARENTING EARLY ADOLESCENCE

As early adolescents experience the move into an adult body, their psychological lives become disrupted by intense and rapidly fluctuating emotions. The containment previously offered by family relationships is challenged by an awareness of feeling outside the family. The mental structures and defences that were established during childhood have to be reorganised in order to accomplish the tasks and aims of adolescence. This process is given momentum by a developmental push into the world outside the family, both in terms of newly developing social relationships and maturing intellectual development.

During puberty the adolescents' relationship to their parents is affected by feelings of ambivalence and insecurity. The manner in which these feelings were handled during earlier periods of development will affect the resources available to the adolescent and parents during puberty. The early adolescents' relationship to their parents can fluctuate rapidly from requiring emergency parental assistance with volatile feelings, closely followed by extreme vulnerability or shame, or the rejection of parents as primary supports.

The parents of adolescents can be faced with a bewildering succession of representations of themselves, which may have less to do with their experience of the reality of themselves as parents and more to do with the internal world of the adolescent. Parents often find themselves drawn into acting out these extreme versions of themselves or struggling not to, and to retain a sense of balance. The parent–child relationship at this time can be extremely demanding for both parties. This close involvement can be understood to be a process of projection of emotions and internal representations from both parties into each other. This process of communication of emotions is based on foundations laid down during the early relationship between the infant and its parents, which has been helpfully described by Bion (1962) in terms of 'container-contained' or the process of containment. When difficult emotions are communicated to a parental figure who can process and manage the feelings provoked, containment is being provided. The adult can then communicate the results of this process to the child, or adolescent, who can internalise this experience, of a containing communicating object, within themselves, which they can begin to rely on when faced with difficult feelings.

This process of communication is crucial for the parenting of adolescents. For both the young adolescent and the parents communication can lead to the containment of fears and anxieties and become an opportunity for anxieties to be managed, modified, and transformed into a new relationship with each other. However, alongside the adolescents' need to utilise their parents as containers for difficult and unwanted feelings, an essential feature of the newly emerging relationship will be an experience of distance and separation. The process of achieving this is often suffused with aggressive feelings towards the parents or carers of the young person.

The demands placed on the parent–child relationship during early adolescence are linked to internal changes taking place at the core of the personality. The close relationship established between the ego and superego during the 'latency' period of childhood is challenged and reorganised during adolescence. As the adolescent begins to separate from his or her parents a corresponding separation takes place internally. The adolescent's diminishing reliance on parental advice is reflected internally by changes taking place in the relationship between the ego and superego. The superego's influence in guiding moral thought and behaviour diminishes, leaving the ego somewhat impoverished, so that when under pressure the adolescent can experience weakness and uncertainty. This can result in a loss of control leading to an outbreak of lawless or delinquent behaviour, which may lead to referral to agencies outside the family. Such behaviour may be rooted in a misdirected search for a love object or in the attraction of escaping from feelings of loneliness and depression caused by the internal shifts during these developments. A young adolescent referred following incidents of stealing at school provided an example of this. He had little insight into what had caused him to steal but was using the profits to buy food and friendship.

As adolescents separate from their parents they depend less on external parental support. This greater independence creates space for the influence of new relationships and the formation of new identifications with peers, other significant adults, and the wider world. Adolescents need their parents to be able to tolerate and encourage the changes within the family. Parents can assist or hinder their adolescents in the moves towards establishing sexual relationships of their own. This development confronts parents with the feelings associated with the Oedipus complex as they find themselves in the position of being on the outside of a sexually active couple.

When the changes in the relationship between parent and adolescent become impossible to negotiate there may be an inhibition in development, for example in cases of agoraphobia, depression, school refusal, the development of eating disorders, or a violent separation enacted by the young person leaving or being forced to leave home.

The difficulties posed by the process of adolescent individuation from a parent's viewpoint was evident in the following clinical example, where my contact with the mother of this 14-year-old girl seen for brief psychotherapy focused on parenting.

Clinical example

Isabel attended a large local comprehensive school. Her mother, Ms. Brown, disapproved of Isabel's friends and had resorted to locking the phone in order to stop her making phone calls. She felt rejected by Isabel and their relationship involved secrets, hidden provocations, deception, physical violence, and lies. It emerged that Ms. Brown's anxieties about separation had been apparent much earlier. She had breast-fed Isabel until she was 4 and did not send her to an ordinary school until she was 8. Ms. Brown was a lone parent with a childhood history that had involved fleeing political persecution and her own mother suffering a disabling illness when Ms. Brown was a toddler.

The parent therapy provided an opportunity for Ms. Brown to understand how her own childhood and adolescence had influenced her relationship with her daughter. She was unable to help her daughter with the adolescent separation process without feeling overwhelming fear and anxiety about losing her completely; she could also no longer bear to be entangled inside the persecuting enmeshed relationship with her daughter resulting from this impasse. In order to escape from these difficulties Ms. Brown felt that Isabel should move away to boarding school and be based in another family.

As Ms. Brown expressed and explored her own fears, and I listened and attended to her overwhelming and confusing emotions, she began to manage to listen to her daughter's point of view. Communication took place between them and Isabel insisted that she wanted to stay at her school. Mrs Brown began to be able to tolerate Isabel's friendships and growing independence and the fears of an emotional disaster receded.

During the course of this therapy, I was impressed by the tenacity of Isabel's adolescent development. In spite of her mother's difficulties she had managed to get to school, where her academic functioning was satisfactory, and had formed peer friendships that she was determined to keep.

SOCIAL DEVELOPMENTS AND INTERNAL CHANGE IN ADOLESCENCE

In the context of a psychoanalytic view of internal changes and identity formation, social developments, which take place outside the family, are crucial to personality development.

Friendships

During adolescence a number of changes take place in social relationships. Boys channel their emerging sexuality into forming significant close friendships and grouping together; at times they separate themselves off from girls, who may become denigrated or objects of contempt. Desired qualities or achievements amongst members of their peer group are idealised so that friendships can be suffused with admiration and love. Behind this the boy is struggling with his need to separate from his own mother, which is represented by his separation from girls in general.

Girls at this stage channel their development into forming distinct same-sex groups, which, unlike the precarious world of primary school groups, are reasonably stable. Girls also develop close one-to-one friendships which, if disrupted, can cause great despair. Deutsch (1946) described the girls' early adolescence in terms of a strong bisexual tendency, which is less repressed than in boys. The idealisation previously described amongst boys' friendships is sometimes manifested by a 'crush' on an older woman, who is loved passively but from whom there is a longing to receive attention and affection. For girls there is a more conscious uncertainty about their gender identity.

One psychoanalytic model of these social developments suggests that failure to participate in these emotionally charged peer group relationships can lead to difficulties in establishing a heterosexual identity (Blos, 1962). The changes, which were described earlier, in the young adolescent's relationship to their internal parents' involved a withdrawal of emotional energy from the parents; this energy is then turned onto the adolescent self. This accounts for the self-absorption and narcissism observed in young adolescents. This uncomfortable state of affairs is offered some relief by peer group relationships which take over from the parental relationship as the centre of meaningful emotional life and identity. These intense peer group relationships provide the adolescent with relationships within which they can express their loving feelings and idealisations.

Friendships formed during adolescence provide the young person with intensely charged relationships that embody aspects of themselves (Copley, 1993). They identify with their friends and these identifications and relationships are then internalised. Through internalisation a varied and complex internal world is built up that provides a widening basis from which more intimate sexual relationships can be formed. When this happens, and the adolescent 'falls in love', there is a dramatic shift as emotional energy is now focused on the boy or girl friend and gratification is looked for and hopefully found within this relationship, rather than from the self.

Groups and gangs

Adolescent peer groups can be dominated by a culture that brings them into violent conflicts with others. Sometimes this leads to the bullying of others who are designated as outside the group or given a scapegoat role within the group. Alternatively there may be fights with other groups of youngsters. Such groups are probably better described as a gang and may be dominated by a fight-flight culture that seeks to avoid the psychologically difficult task of thinking (Bion, 1961). The following brief description of my work with Rick illustrates some aspects of this form of adolescent peer culture.

Clinical example

Rick was 14 years old, and he attended a school dominated by inter-racial gang formation. It was his struggle with this kind of group culture that he brought to his therapy. He was a strong and successful sportsman and it seemed possible that his ambition to become a professional in his sport could succeed. However he was prone to violent confrontation when he felt unjustly treated and was frequently involved in aggressive confrontations with teachers. His sensitivity to these situations was intensified by his experience of racism, which he vigorously confronted.

Rick was drawn into the schools fight-flight culture and found himself swept away by the terrifying but thrilling sense of omnip-otence which can fuel these groups when a conflict takes place. A disagreement, or cuss, leads to a fight, which develops into a powerful escalation in the minds of the youngsters; brothers will be called in as reinforcements, followed by cousins and their associates from distant cities. At times this turns into a reality as gangs form.

The problem we faced was to recognise, understand, and express the intense fear Rick experienced as he was swept into this process. We were helped by the reality of the consequences of gang violence, which tragically have resulted in the death of a pupil in his neighbour-hood. We also had to acknowledge his need to feel part of, and therefore protected by, the 'fighting' group identity. Rick felt trapped by the necessity to be part of the gang culture, which dominated the community he lived in, and was able to articulate his frustration about feeling that he had no alternative but to take his part. Fight-flight groups make it hard for the individual members to think about and develop their own thoughts based on the reality of their emotional experience.

In the case of Rick his sporting achievements allowed him space and support for his emerging individuality. A similar situation is dramatised in the film 'Saturday Night Fever' in which the character Tony, played by John Travolta, is a talented dancer. In order to enter dance competitions, he rehearsed with a girl to whom he became attracted. This developing relationship took place against the backdrop of his membership of a delinquent 'thrill seeking' male adolescent gang. The film climaxes with his struggle to leave the gang and move on to an intimate heterosexual relationship.

Thinking about delinquency

Increasing numbers of children and adolescents are involved in delinquent activities; the range of offences varies widely, as do the reasons why young people offend. Being part of a gang, involved in the thrills and excitement of risk-taking, propels some into acting out. For others taking drugs can become compulsive, or develop into an addiction—the need to finance drug consumption can lead to a vicious circle of delinquent activities. Delinquent acting out may be a way of getting back at a society from which they feel excluded, or may indicate more longstanding emotional problems. There is clear evidence that gender differences influence delinquent acting out, young males being much more prone to delinquency than young women.

The complex roots of such activities are illustrated by a case reported by Hindle (1998). She described working with a 16-year-old boy, Chris, who, following his father's suicide, was referred to the Child and Adolescent Psychiatry Unit. The family had been known to Social Services and had intermittent contact with Adult Mental Health Services. Chris's father was a heavy drinker and reports were made of marital problems and domestic violence. Following his father's death Chris disclosed that he had been both physically and sexually abused by his father. Chris fluctuated between blaming himself for what had happened and claiming he was glad that his father was dead. Some months later Chris was prosecuted for stealing power tools that he had stored, but not sold on. Hindle viewed Chris's offending as symbolic of his internal dilemmas—his feelings of triumph in relation to his father's death, his wish for power (the tools) and the ability to defend himself, and yet his inability to use the stolen tools, underlining his sense of fear and powerlessness. When Chris was imprisoned for this offence, his punishment became muddled with unconscious feelings of guilt about his father's death.

The emotional roots of offending behaviour are explored by Cordess and Williams (1996), who state that a 'previous emotionally unbearable traumatic experience may erupt into offensive action if it has remained "split off" and psychologically speaking has remained "undigested" or "unmetabolised"'. This above case illustrates how the youth justice service, which focuses on offending, may find it difficult to address the complex developmental and mental health issues underlying such behaviour.

Mid-adolescence

It is helpful to identify two broad emotional themes as dominant during mid-adolescence. One theme is 'being in love', as new relationships are established and internalised. The second theme is 'mourning', which relates to the childhood relationship to the 'internal parental objects' being relinquished and a new one established. The concept of mourning seems to be a suitable starting point for describing mid-adolescence because it emphasises the immense emotional demands associated with this phase of development. Successful mourning is an intensely painful mental process leading to the separation of the self and the object via a gradual process of reversing the links between the self and the object (Freud, 1917/1961i). This leads to a changed relationship in which the object is viewed more realistically, and the ego is enriched.

This description can be applied to the process of internal development the adolescent has to engage in, as the separation from childhood-based internalised parents involves a gradual process of separation from, and mourning for, earlier versions of the parent–child relationship and the establishment of a more realistically based relationship. Just as successful mourning leads to internal ego enrichment, so adolescent development establishes an enriched internal environment.

During the mid-adolescent period this enrichment is evident in a deepening and intensification of emotional life. Early adolescent strivings, which lead to a break from internal infantile object ties, result in a build-up of emotional energy focused on the self. This causes increasing self-absorption and a diminished ability to test reality. The adolescent feels estranged from his or her familiar childhood relationships but experiences a strong need and desire for new attachments and identifications that will express and embellish their emotional life. This appetite for good relationships and new identifications helps the adolescents build up a sense of self-esteem and self-importance. Intense but often superficial and transitory relationships to people, causes, or ideas are formed.

Internally a battle is being fought against regression. The adolescents' unconscious absorption with establishing their own sexual identity stimulates an awareness of, and curiosity about, their parents' sexual life. This is vigorously defended against and may be transformed into an attacking and critical view of parental inadequacy and failure. During this period parents face difficult and unpleasant feelings as they can become degraded figures towards whom the young person feels rebellious and defiant. The adolescent becomes increasingly involved with close groups of friends, which tend to move on from the same-sex groupings of younger years to mixed groups with fluctuating allegiances and affections.

The adolescent's internal experience of isolation is mitigated by a rich daydreaming fantasy life in which they may represent themselves in an idealised role. This can be thought of as a rehearsal for the relationship to the real world. At times this internal life is expressed in terms of make-believe relationships that encompass the adolescent's emotional needs and help in the disengagement from parental ties. This highly energised internal life can create an acute sensory sensitivity to the world, which may be shared with fellow travellers or expressed in artistic endeavours.

Idealisation is an important part of the adolescent defensive armour as it assists the build-up of a good internal object. However, idealisation is almost always accompanied by denigration. During adolescence it is usually the unwanted and dependent aspects of identity that are denigrated and pushed aside. These unwanted parts of the self may be projected into parents or other available adult authority figures who, in response, may feel that they are hopeless failures.

For some young people the failure to establish a sufficiently robust internal good object during earlier development leaves them without a good enough object to identify with and nurture during adolescence. Their self-absorption may focus on a hatred and loathing of themselves and their bodies. A mixture of these two aspects of emotional life is present in the minds of all adolescents. If a balanced adult is to emerge, some integration of these extremes must be achieved.

The following clinical example illustrates some of the difficulties that arose for an adolescent who had a poorly established good internal object. His social needs were frustrated when he experienced problems with friendships and this led to him becoming preoccupied by self-destructive feelings.

Clinical example

John was advised to seek counselling by his doctor, whom he had consulted because he felt depressed. He told the doctor that he had been having fantasies about killing himself. I met a self-absorbed, anxious-looking John who was able to tell me that his suicidal thoughts involved a violent or explosive death by shooting or jumping off a building. John was unable to offer any connection these ideas might have to his personal history.

John was the youngest of four children of a professional and educated couple. John himself had achieved excellent GCSE results and was now taking A levels but he was underachieving and in danger of failing. He did feel that the transfer into 6th form had been traumatic and that he had become withdrawn and depressed because his peer group relationships had changed and he could not relate to his 'subject' mates.

I gradually established that John's suicidal thoughts had begun when he was 14. This was connected to his late physical development, which made it difficult for him to retain a place in his peer group and made him lose confidence. He was the victim of some bullying and had anxiously tried to placate his tormentors. At one point his loneliness impelled him to seek friendship with a boy who he himself had bullied and excluded at both primary and secondary school.

The anger and distress that he felt about these experiences, and his shame about his late pubertal development, led him to withdraw into a private retreat. He expressed his feelings of rage and shame in his suicidal fantasies, which gave vent to his aggression and also provided him with an escape into a powerful version of himself. He found it difficult to talk to his parents about these difficulties; like many adolescents he was trying to manage these problems on his own.

After some months of regular appointments, John's suicidal thoughts began to recede. He was able to tell me about his use of drugs of various kinds and to realise that this self-prescribed medication increased rather than alleviated his depression. He struggled to manage periods of intense depression during which he felt isolated and unable to function intellectually or socially. He began to express, accept, and integrate his negative feelings about himself and his relationships, and to take more responsibility for looking after his talents and intelligence.

John's difficulties were expressed on two fronts. Internally he was unable to establish and sustain a positive relationship with his developing mind and body and this was reflected in his external relationships. His over-riding need to find a place in a peer group made it difficult for him to function on the basis of his feelings, and this exacerbated the split between his social persona and his inner emotional world.

Adolescent groups

As I have already indicated, for both boys and girls, friendship groups allow them to explore aspects of their own personalities. Individuals within the groups are significant for different reasons, e.g. the baby, the humorist, the arguer, the victim, and these different roles represent aspects of the individual participants' complex emerging personalities. These differences are explored within the safety of the agreed rules of an adolescent community that specifies adherence to certain music, fashion, speech, and culture.

Some post-Kleinian theorists have suggested that this adolescent community offers a container for development based on an 'adhesive identification', which is a defensive manoeuvre taken in order to avoid fears of spilling out or falling into space (Copley, 1993; Meltzer, 1973). These are primitive infantile fears that are experienced by young infants and reappear with the upheavals of adolescence.

Adhesive identification was first described by Bick (1968, 1986), as a feature of infants who have had insufficient maternal containment and so are unable to develop sufficient internal identifications with a parental presence. A sufficient mother–child relationship provides the infant with an experience of a 'second skin' which holds together the unintegrated parts of the self. If the maternal relationship fails to provide a second skin, infants may form a superficial skin in its place, which is based on an 'adhesive identification'. This is formed by sticking, or adhering, to surface features of their experience in order to try to create an experience of a container, or skin.

Copley (1993) uses the concept of 'adhesive identification' to explain adolescent groupings that hold themselves together in 'an adhesive sticky manner, making—and adhering to—its own changing culture of clothes, music and speech, and thus forming its own identity card; we skin container'. Copley suggests that this 'we' skin container may help to mark a boundary that provides a sense of safety from intergenerational hostility.   *so dated*

The contemporary 'rave ecstasy' culture provides us with an example of adhesive identification. Raves offer young people an exhilarating experience of boundaryless belonging, which I think of as the ultimate manic defence. The purpose of a manic defence is to deny the awareness of exclusion, loneliness, or rejection and its attendant emotions. A young person's ability to integrate this denied aspect of their internal experience, and to recover from the comedown from the ecstasy high, is placed under great stress by repeated exposures to the rave lifestyle.

The concept of adhesive identification helps us to think about features of adolescent groups and culture and to relate the distinct identity formed by successive generations of adolescents to the presence of intense infantile anxieties. However, these ideas may not account sufficiently for the role of adolescent groups in facilitating creativity and nurturing the new ideas, opinions, and values that individuals identify with 'their' generation.

A common theme emerging out of adolescence is the feeling of danger associated with being an outsider (Dartington, 1994). For all adolescents the membership of a group or gang assuages the experience of being an outsider and provides a social experience that assists the development of a personal identity.

In late adolescence, the fact that the young person takes up an outsider's position in relation to his or her family assists the possibility of forming a therapeutic alliance. This stance is often experienced as a crisis for the adolescent's family as they are confronted by the adolescent utilising their intellect, and adopting the role of 'a seeker of the truth', to criticise their parents' generation. Dartington (1994) explores this aspect of the move to adulthood, which she names the phase of 'necessary scepticism'. She regards this phase as essential for healthy individuation as it enables the adolescent to 'throw off the mantle of various assumed identities'. This is only possible if the family can withdraw their own projections into the young person and tolerate having an outsider in their midst.

Leaving home

In late adolescence the young person's identity as an 'outsider' within the family leads to thoughts about leaving home. The process of negotiating this move is influenced by a variety of factors including the young person's internal resources, the progress of their social and intellectual development, the familial and parental capacities to assist this transition, and the influence of external circumstances.

The end of secondary school marks the 'end of an era' for most adolescents. Groups of friends fragment as individuals take up opportunities available to them and move off in different directions. Some young people can be left behind and isolated. Their wish to leave home and move on can be at odds with what is realistically available. At this stage they may fall through the net of services or may be unable to access services that could assist them.

For others, leaving home is negotiated in a planned way as the young person gathers their financial resources in order to manage independently. Academic achievement at school may result in a move away from home associated with further education (as described in Chapter 9). Social achievements of adolescence can assist young people who leave home to live with a group of friends in shared accommodation. Still others may form intimate partnerships or marry, leaving one family in order to form another.

In the family the feelings surrounding these events are usually intense, but the tensions and anxieties associated with separation can be followed by feelings of relief. Whatever the circumstances, when one member of the family leaves home it involves a major readjustment for all its members. Younger siblings may miss their older brother or sister or discover a new-found confidence as the 'oldest' child in the family. Parents, who may be intimately involved in supporting this transition, are often confronted by the changes that have taken place in social and economic circumstances since their own adolescence. An 'empty nest' can generate a new lease of life for some parents as they have the time and freedom to develop and rediscover their own interests. A parental couple may respond to these changes by renegotiating their relationship with each other—this may result in a strengthening of their relationship or it may highlight difficulties for those who have invested in their children, but grown apart from each other.

For some adolescents the difficulty in finding employment, or employment that pays sufficiently to enable economic independence, can lead to intense frustration and feelings of despair. Unemployment perpetuates their dependence on their parents at a time when they are struggling to establish an identity and role for themselves in the world outside the family. This can be particularly painful if the parents are facing unemployment or redundancy themselves.

For many adolescents, remaining at home is the only option. Home can provide a base from which they study at college or university, often combining this with part-time work. The financial contribution that a young person can make towards the household may facilitate the process of growing independence or it may cause tensions, difficulties, and arguments. In this situation parents too ready with advice or criticism may cause additional pain to adolescents struggling to face disappointments and a future with limited prospects. It is not uncommon for these problems to emerge after a period of successful separation; young adults often return home at the end of a period of further education, or because a relationship doesn't work out, or for other reasons.

Sexual relationships and social conformity

It is a fact that for the majority, the outcome and expected outcome of establishing a sexual identity is expressed in heterosexual relationships. A significant minority of adolescents, however, are aware of different identities and experience homosexual or bisexual fantasies that can lead into real relationships and the establishment of a bisexual or homosexual identity. Although significant changes in social attitudes have occurred, and many young people themselves are aware of this, in my clinical experience homosexual thoughts and experiences cause great anxiety and confusion for most adolescents and this can lead to difficulty in having meaningful sexual relationships and establishing a contented sense of sexual identity.

For most young people there is a strong need for the turmoil of adolescence to be resolved by an experience of a satisfying and meaningful sexual relationship and many seek therapeutic help when this is not realised. Relationships that have been formed may have been based on an unconscious wish to take revenge on parents or to re-enact earlier relationships that have not been emotionally processed. Of course this doesn't stop with adolescence, but often contributes to difficulties experienced during adult relationships as well.

The social and internal pressures to conform results in some adolescents appearing to perform normally but being unable to integrate their identity internally. This can be manifested in a confused state, reflected in an inability to cope with the normal demands of life. The pressures of social conformity may be intensified by cultural conflicts, which can result in particular pressures for the adolescent in second- or third-generation immigrant families.

The problems adolescents have in progressing into satisfactory sexual relationships commonly relate to a failure to work through the emotional ties to parental figures. Disruptions in family life caused by death, divorce, unhappy marriages, mental or physical illness, poverty, and physical or sexual abuse make the task of separating from internal and external ties extremely difficult. For the adolescent or young adult who finds their way to therapeutic help this becomes the focus of the engagement and offers an opportunity to experience and think about feelings and relationships that were ignored, glossed over, denied, or too painful for the family to manage.

For the late adolescent, anxieties about their future and an awareness of unresolved difficulties in relation to his or her family can combine to form a motivation to seek professional help from a psychotherapist or counsellor. Psychotherapists working with this age group find that this motivation assists the possibility of forming a therapeutic alliance that improves the outcome of the treatment. The availability of appropriate and accessible services targeted for late adolescents and young adults is limited, but there is increasing awareness of the need for services to meet the special needs of this age group.

CONCLUSION

The gradual emergence of an individual or personal identity is the hallmark of adolescent development. This involves many changes in the internal emotional life of adolescents within the context of intellectual, familial, and social development, and is linked to a process of separation from the childhood relationships with parents.

For adolescents who are inhibited and unable to progress, therapeutic help may facilitate 'moving on' and engaging in the struggle to be independent and responsible, so often at odds with the regressive wish to remain dependent.

Chapter 8

The transition from late adolescence to young adulthood: Oedipal themes

Lynda Miller

The central emotional issue in late adolescence can be thought of as finding a sense of identity in relation to the parents. Whereas in the early and middle teenage years young people have to separate themselves from their parents in order to establish an identity of their own, as they approach adulthood their relationship to the parents has to be renegotiated. For a young person to begin to feel that he or she is an adult, it is necessary to have internal parental figures with whom to identify.

This process can be conceptualised usefully in an Oedipal framework. This lecture links together clinical experience and theoretical formulations in a way which I hope will be helpful in thinking about this age group.

I want to begin with a quote from Rey (1994) concerning the use of the term Oedipus complex in psychoanalytic literature:

> The vital process that drives men and women to each other, to love each other and then create life, and thus achieve the continuation of the human race Freud called the Oedipus complex. In a way he has created a double-edged problem, for this life activity was thus not only described as the most important psychobiological undertaking of human beings, but also it was transferred to the realm of mythology around the Oedipus complex ... Was it a so-called scientific theory, or had it become a part of mythology? Or was it both?

Rey is drawing attention to the danger of using the term Oedipus complex to mystify, to place beyond the realm of ordinary human understanding, this process with which we are all familiar—the sexual attraction between men and women that is essential for the survival of the species. It is inborn, part of us from the beginning, so it is not surprising that it manifests in a primitive form in early childhood. Given that we are very complex, varied, and sensitive creatures, it is also not surprising that in reality the development of the Oedipus complex is often neither simple nor problem-free.

Keeping Rey's point in mind places the Oedipus complex, as Freud certainly placed it, in the psychobiological realm; as such it can be thought of as a universal developmental process and one that engages us throughout our life span. The struggle to move on from our intense primary emotional relationships with our parents, to the possibilities of other relationships with partners, work, children, creative activities, and the wider realms of human experience, is the focus of this lecture. For many young people, this can become a crisis at the time when it is socially expected that they will make the transition from adolescence to adulthood.

EXTERNAL AND INTERNAL PERSPECTIVES

By late adolescence the major bodily and hormonal changes of puberty are probably complete, and in Western society many young people will have left, or be in process of leaving, the parental home. The relationship with parents, which in childhood had strong components of dependency and obedience, will also have changed. Throughout adolescence, the peer group gains in significance, and from a psychoanalytic perspective is important in its function of identity formation. As described in the previous chapter, young people 'lend and borrow' aspects of themselves to each other, through unconscious processes of projection and introjection.

In later adolescence, future adult responsibilities begin to impinge. For some, further education both extends this stage of development and provides preparation or qualification for employment. For others, leaving school coincides with entering the world of work. Late adolescents and young adults may go into work at different points and for different reasons. For some, the wish to earn money and to become independent is an over-riding desire. Others may follow the 'family tradition' by seeking work in a particular industry or field. Others still may have little choice, having to take what is available, perhaps on a temporary basis. Others may be fortunate enough to discover an area of work that captures their interest and imagination. The capacity to manage in the workplace rests upon the achievement of a degree of emotional maturity. Qualities such as self-motivation and being able to cooperate and to work with others are called upon. Finding one's place in a different kind of structure from that which characterises educational settings involves tolerating a new kind of authority and discipline, whether the post is relatively senior or junior. Learning new tasks may require forfeiting some previous ways of knowing, and may necessitate a struggle to acquire new competencies and skills. Being able to work is a lynchpin of the adult world. For those unable to establish themselves in work, for whatever reason, unemployment and possible homelessness loom ahead.

Although external factors influence this stage of development, internally the transition from late adolescence to early adulthood is more subtle and complex. Social conformity may betray a superficial adaptation to adult expectations, but the gradual internal changes necessary to feel genuinely able to embrace one's adulthood may be part of a hard-won process, not necessarily located in the early 20s. Indeed, as apparent adults, we all have infantile, child-like, and adolescent aspects of ourselves.

From a psychoanalytic developmental perspective, the relationship with the internal parents is of central importance at this point in life. Copley (1993) describes the re-establishment of internal relationships as a central force in emotional life in this way:

> Introjective identification ... with loved internal parental objects, in both their masculine and feminine roles, is intrinsic to the formation and maintenance of a mature adult state of mind.

It may be helpful here to differentiate introjective identification, a developmental learning process, from projective identification. In the latter mode of functioning, the young person would be 'jumping into the parents' shoes' so would in a sense be acting as an adult without having matured inwardly; one could say becoming a 'pseudo-adult'. Introjective processes involve a gradual taking in of admired parental qualities, a learning through experience, and this rests upon respect and concern for the actual parents. As adolescents are usually set against their parents to some extent, in order to define themselves, this usually involves forgiveness of parents for their perceived faults (real and imagined) and a coming to terms with their different values and ideas. Introjective identification is a gradual, maturational process in which the separate identity of the other is recognised, whereas projective identification is based upon the wish to take over the identity of another, for motives such as control or envy.

If development towards maturity progresses healthily (and this does not mean without the pain and anxiety related to separation), the sense of self as a separate individual is strengthened, and dependency upon parents and peer group diminishes. It is this separate sense of self that allows mature adult relationships to develop; a loving, sexual relationship with a partner, the possibility of parenthood, an interest in the world with concern for suffering, a friendly, mutually respectful relationship with parents. Not all of these may be achieved, but that which underlies all of them is essential; the firm establishment of good relationships with one's internal objects, where loving feelings predominate over hate.

Development is rarely a problem-free process and throughout life one has to struggle with conflicting feelings towards others. At this point of transition to adulthood, the struggle may be particularly intense, because the infantile part of the self clings in phantasy to a controlling, sexualised relationship with the internal parents. Externally, this may take the form of prolonged dependence upon the actual parents, and difficulties in making new relationships with sexual partners. Where infantile tendencies predominate, unrealistic expectations of the sexual partner, such as excessive demands for attention or irrational jealousy, may threaten to spoil new relationships.

This struggle to become an adult can be fraught and painful; if the adolescent is to emerge as an individual young person with a firm sense of self and a capacity to make new and fulfilling relationships in the adult world, the intense infantile needs and desires experienced towards the parents in childhood have to be worked through.

PHANTASY AND REALITY

Throughout his life as an extraordinarily creative thinker and prolific writer, Freud inevitably changed and developed his ideas, sometimes giving rise to radical theoretical shifts. However, he consistently maintained a deep interest in the relationship between the internal life of human beings, in particular unconscious processes, and the external life of events consciously experienced and remembered.

It is not useful, nor is it true to Freud's ideas, to say that at one point he attributed neurotic illness solely to actual traumatic events, then at a later date solely to unconscious phantasies. His interest lay in the relationship between the unconscious and life events; for example, what happens to memories when they are subjected to unconscious processes such as repression, condensation, and displacement and emerge in symbolic form in dreams?

Broadly speaking, it could be said that Freud first held the view that neuroses could be traced back to repressed memories, subject to distortion in the unconscious, of traumatic experiences, in particular those which we would now call sexual abuse. He believed that servants, such as nurses and nannies, of middle-class children, regularly abused the children in their care. This came to be known as Freud's childhood seduction theory. It has been revived recently in a much-publicised book by Masson (1989), who criticised Freud for departing from this view.

Through his own self-analysis, especially analysis of his own dreams, Freud came to the realisation that the notion of childhood seduction has a strong component of phantasy, generated by unconscious wishes. He did not deny the possibility of the reality of actual seduction of children by adults, although he has been accused, as by Masson, of doing so. This debate is contemporary, for example in instances where people in psychotherapy claim to have been put in touch with repressed memories of childhood abuse, and turn against their parents. The debate of whether one is dealing with phantasy or reality continues.

Stanton (1994) wrote the following about this issue:

> In fact, Freud never had a seduction theory in the sense that Masson claims, and was always concerned with the complex nature of traumatic experience. Even in Freud's early letters to his friend Fliess ... Freud is concerned with the way in

which unconscious material fundamentally transforms and vit-
iates the capacity to remember.

Freud's self-analysis, the keystone to his formulation of psychoanalytic ideas, is partially evidenced in his letters to Fliess. In 1897
Freud recognised that his own memories of 'infatuation with the
mother and jealousy of the father' referred to 'a general event in
early childhood'. He wrote to Fliess that the Oedipal relationship
of the child to its parents might explain the gripping power of
Oedipus Rex.

As a highly cultured European, Freud was deeply interested
and well versed in classical mythology. He began to develop the
idea that myths are endopsychic, or internally generated, and as
such underlie the narratives of literature and religion, revealing
unconscious psychological truths about the human mind.

In *The interpretation of dreams* (1899/1961c) Freud elaborated
upon the Oedipus complex without naming it as such. He stated
the view that 'being in love with one and hating the other part
of the parental pair' not only pertains to neurotics but to all
human beings.

By 1905, in *Three essays on sexuality* Freud (1905/1961d) clearly
held the view that children are endowed with sexual feelings, and
a more complicated formulation of the Oedipus complex gradually
unfolded in his mind. Later, he named the Oedipus complex
definitively, and designated it the 'nuclear complex' of the
neuroses.

The Oedipus myth grew out of folklore tales passed on in the
oral tradition in Greece. The Greek dramatists formulated these
tales as tragic plays to be performed at religious festivals to Diony-
sius. *Oedipus Rex* is part of a trilogy of plays by Sophocles, and
the story rests upon a prophecy that Oedipus will slay his father
and marry his mother. All attempts to divert the fulfilment of the
prophecy fail; Oedipus unwittingly kills his father, marries his
mother, and when the truth is realised, the play culminates in
tragedy; Jocasta, his mother, kills herself, and Oedipus blinds
himself.

In Steiner's paper (1985) *Turning a blind eye: The cover-up for
Oedipus*, the theme of blinding is explored in terms of choosing
not to see, the defence of denial. Choosing to see, on the other
hand, could be called insight into the unconscious. Then there is
a choice between development in accord with the reality principle,

with all its frustrations, or denial of reality to avoid frustration, which leads to the enactment of unconscious phantasy.

Following on from his insight into the nature of unconscious phantasy through his self-analysis, Freud tended to swing away from the so-called childhood seduction theory. In the case of Dora (Freud, 1905/1961e), an 18-year-old girl whom Freud treated for a period of 11 weeks in the year 1900, his emphasis is so strongly upon wish-fulfilling phantasy that he gives little weight to the inappropriate treatment of Dora by the adults in her life. In contrast, in the case study commonly referred to as the Wolf Man, Freud (1918/1961j) is able to give more weight to external reality, i.e. the disturbing effects upon a child of witnessing parental intercourse, and links this with unconscious phantasy.

In the clinical material that follows I hope to give a picture of the transitional period between adolescence and adulthood, when Oedipal issues press for resolution, manifesting in various forms of emotional disturbance.

Such clinical material is derived from my work in a University Student Counselling Service in a town in the home counties. Most of the students are self-referred, although sometimes a tutor or lecturer will have suggested that they contact the counselling service. They are usually undergraduates, aged from 18 to 30, and occasionally older. The students are from diverse backgrounds, and a considerable number are from overseas.

CULTURAL AND SEXUAL ISSUES

As young people struggle towards finding an adult identity, areas of conflict that frequently arise concern their cultural and sexual identifications. I will give an example of each below.

Clinical example

Ali is a student in his early twenties, from a wealthy Asian family, resident in the U.K. Ali came to the counselling service complaining of terrible headaches, which prevented him from studying and sleeping. He spoke of picturing scenes of violence in his mind, which frightened and upset him.

Ali told me that his parents expected him to join the family business on completion of his studies, but Ali was unsure whether or not he wanted this. He said that he would have liked to have taken a course in theatre design rather than business studies, but this was unacceptable to his father. He described life at home as characterised by loud arguments between his parents, and he could not understand why they stayed together. He sympathised with his mother, whom he felt was badly treated by his father.

Ali took his therapy sessions seriously and seemed to be making progress. His headaches disappeared and he began to be able to think with me about his conflict concerning his studies and the plans for his future.

During the course of the therapy Ali became attracted to an older woman in his course, and I felt that this had transference implications. After some weeks of fantasising about her in his sessions, he spoke to her one evening and then spent the night in her flat. Ali came to his next session expressing disgust at himself for this, and said that he had no desire for further sexual contact with this woman.

Soon after this incident Ali took a long holiday with his uncle in his home country. Ali returned from this holiday to tell me that his uncle had advised him well and that he now felt happy to study in order to enter the family business.

In this case, as with many others, I had tried to keep in mind the complex cultural issues which were interwoven with Ali's difficulties. I knew that Ali was under strong familial and cultural pressure to follow the expected path for male children. However, as Ali broke off his therapy at the same time as making this decision, I felt that the opportunity afforded by therapy for Ali to look at his conflicting feelings had proved too difficult for him to sustain. His manner towards me in his final session was somewhat disdainful, and I think this could be understood in terms of Ali's identification with the father/uncle who treats the mother/older woman/therapist badly.

For Ali, an Oedipal resolution of allowing the parental couple to come together in his mind (one could express this as the integration of his feminine, creative nature with his masculine, logical side) was impossible to achieve, at least at this point in his life.

Clinical example

Gina, an Italian student aged 19 years, came to the counselling service because of difficulties in her relationships. She told me immediately that she was gay, but that this in itself was not a problem. Rather, she said that she yearned for a serious, long-term committed relationship with a woman, but each time she became close to someone, it all seemed to go wrong.

Gina told me that her father had died suddenly when she was 12 years old. She had been very close to him, and all the family were devastated by the loss. Gina was the oldest child of a large family and described herself as practical, and as having 'a good head for figures', even at that age. She was studying for a degree in maths.

She said that she took on her father's role in the family as her mother was not a practical person at all, and had relied on her husband to take responsibility for the family bills. However, in the relationships she described with women friends, she was far from rational and capable. Gina was an insightful young woman, and was quickly able to realise that she brought to these relationships an intense emotional neediness and a jealous possessiveness that made the other person feel trapped and overwhelmed.

In the therapy it was possible to explore with Gina the ways in which her 12-year-old emotional needs were still pressing to be met. She was gradually able to contain these feelings within herself (through expressing them in the therapy and experiencing containment in the therapeutic setting) and to allow relationships in the outside world to develop at an easier pace.

Her sexual orientation did not come into question throughout the course of the therapy. In Gina's case the task was to differentiate her infantile needs (to possess the mother exclusively) from her more mature desires for friendship and sexual relationships.

INTEGRATION AND IDENTITY

Many of the students who come to the counselling service for help are struggling with developmental tasks that fall within the 'normal' range. After a few sessions they feel that they can carry on with their lives and their studies and have no further need for help. Predominant issues centre on the difficulties of leaving home and separating from the family, involving feelings of loss and anxiety. When these feelings are confronted and thought about they usually begin to seem more manageable.

Quite frequently adolescents in this age-group are able to make good use of brief therapeutic work, probably because it is a time in life when the need to find an identity in the adult world begins to press urgently. Student life can still feel like a protected space where 'others' are the adults with responsibilities. Indeed, the student–lecturer relationship has child–parent connotations, where the emphasis is on the student learning from those who have more knowledge and experience.

This is also a time, if real learning is taking place, when students are developing capacities to think for themselves, formulate their own ideas, and write about them in course work and examinations. This can be a crisis for those who have not developed a sense of a separate self, and student counselling services are usually flooded with 'emergencies' during the exam period.

Vulnerable young people of this age group may need help in learning to tolerate their own feelings: feelings of loss of identity as a child in a dependent relationship to the parents, and feelings of anxiety about having to form new relationships as an independent young adult. These feelings are generated by an internal momentum towards growth and development, but if feelings of loss and of anxiety are too intensely painful and overwhelming, young people may get 'stuck.' They cannot move backwards into a child-like dependent state, yet neither do they feel able to move forwards and become separate.

For most young people these internal struggles may never be evident on the 'outside', and they find their way through the impasse. Others may need help in trying to understand what is impeding them from moving forwards into adulthood. An exploration of the unconscious factors that contribute to the difficulties characteristic of late adolescence and approaching adulthood reveals that in various forms, Oedipal themes emerge over and over again, with young people struggling with conflicting feelings towards their parents. Until these are explored and there is a move towards integration, development is impeded.

The emergent self may still be entangled with the internal parents and may not be experienced as being 'free' to think and

to study. Where anger and resentment towards the parents pre-
dominates, it is difficult for the young person to find a basis for
adult identification.

Clinical example

Mary, a social sciences student, is aged 26 years and comes from the
North of England, but her family are of Eastern European origin. She
is an attractive young woman, but extremely tense. She holds herself
rigidly, and a knot of tension is clearly visible on her forehead. Often
her hands are tightly clenched. She referred herself to the counselling
service because she could neither concentrate nor study, and was
getting very behind in her course work.

The first time I met Mary I encountered a thin, tall, pale young
woman with long, unkempt fair hair, dressed in a crumpled careless
way and looking far from well. She told me that she was very
depressed and had problems sleeping; she took a prescription for
anti-depressants out of her bag to show me, as if I would not
otherwise take in the seriousness of what she was telling me.

When I commented on this, she told me that she did not expect
counselling to help her; she had studied all this herself, and did not
believe in it. She said this with an air of defiance, and this, coupled
with the way in which she held her body so rigidly, made me wonder
about a relationship in her mind between a child who does not
expect to be understood, and a mother who fails to understand her,
throwing the child back on to omnipotence as her only means of
holding herself together.

As soon as I had put this thought into words, Mary became very
emotional and expressive, telling me that she had been awoken last
night by a dream which gave her a pain 'here' (she pointed to her
chest) and she could not stop crying. She did not proceed to tell
me about the dream, so I suggested that as it had preceded her first
appointment with me, it may be linked to her anxieties about seeing
a therapist, and her fear, already expressed, that I would not be able
to help her.

With some reluctance, Mary began to relate the dream as follows:

There was a small girl in a foreign country—in the Far East, being driven along in a small carriage, with two seats facing each other. The child is being 'framed' between the seats, as a decoration. (She indicated with her hands that she meant stretched out, as if she were a picture in a frame.) It was horrible. I stood by watching, unable to help. I could see a nail being driven through the child's finger. It was horrible.

By the time she had finished telling me this, Mary was crying, gasping for breath, as if the dream was very vivid to her in the present moment. Indeed, her way of describing the dream made it vivid to me as well, the imagery being strange and powerful.

Clearly there is a child part of Mary who is suffering, in pain, and in urgent need of help. Mary identifies herself in the dream as being unable to get help, a fear already voiced at the beginning of the session.

It was possible to suggest some associative links to the imagery of the dream as Mary was too upset to speak: the Far East may link with Mary's parents' country of origin, East of here and far away in time. The nail driven into the hand may have both religious and sexual connotations in connection with Mary's strict religious upbringing. The child being stretched between the two seats of the carriage suggests a position between the two parents, an Oedipal situation, or even possible sexual abuse given the penetrating nail and 'horribleness' of affect. However, the image of the frame seemed to be the most bizarre and disturbing element of the dream. It raises a question of whether Mary felt herself to be in some way 'framed' in the sense of 'set-up' by her parents, to carry guilt for a deed she had not committed.

When I talked with Mary about this child part of herself which is in great distress, and which Mary feels unable to help by herself, she was both moved and defensive. She told me that she is strong, and wants to be able to help herself, she does not like 'this' (indicating with a sweeping arm gesture the room with me and her in it), yet at the same time she was crying and her eyes and expression were pleading and desperate.

We were only halfway through the first session but the emotional pitch was intense, a strong highly ambivalent transference was evident, and we had pitched headlong into the unconscious via Mary's dream.

I asked about her family background and Mary told me that her mother is intuitive but has no education. Mary has always been very close to her father, she is his favourite, the eldest of three children, but he is cruel and cold to her mother. He had wanted Mary to stay at home and then to get married, do housework and have a family, although he did not actually prevent her from leaving home.

This enabled us to spend the remainder of the session exploring Mary's difficulty in studying. I was left with an impression of a complex internal scenario with Mary indeed placed between her parents, as in the dream. Her problem in studying, which we clarified was so serious as to jeopardise her chances of completing her degree, seemed related to unresolved Oedipal conflicts, preventing her internally from separating from her parents and allowing them to be a couple in her mind.

In subsequent sessions a fuller picture emerged. The second session began with Mary describing another 'terrible' dream, as follows:

My mother was running after me, shooting at me with a gun, with tiny bullets, trying to kill me. Even in the dream this was real and not real at the same time; the bullets did not actually kill me.

When we explored why Mary might dream that her mother was trying to kill her, Mary told me that her younger sister is mother's favourite, and always has been. She related a recent incident from her last visit home when she had overheard her mother giving a special birthday present to her sister, and they had both agreed to keep this a secret from Mary.

The theme of favouritism and jealousy was then further elaborated. Mary perceived herself as her father's favourite and her mother as having always been intensely jealous of the relationship between Mary and her father. There had been problems in the parents' marriage throughout Mary's childhood (she had been witness to many serious rows) culminating in a divorce 3 years ago. As Mary told me this she became extremely agitated and distressed; her hands shaking and patting at her chest as if she could hardly breathe.

I said that it seemed she felt responsible for the divorce, and Mary said that at the time it happened she had found it unbearable and had had a nervous breakdown. She described this as fainting in the street and being taken into hospital unconscious.

I talked about a little child part of herself who feels terribly powerful; as if she really believes that she caused the problems in her parents' marriage by coming between them, like the little girl between the two seats in the dream of the previous week. However, the idea of being framed suggests more that she unconsciously knew that she had been put in the position of being the focus of the parents' problems, and this was not her choice at all.

Mary stopped crying and listened to this carefully. After a silence she said that if that was so, why does she still feel so guilty?

The dream of her mother shooting her indeed suggests guilt, revenge, and punishment, yet the 'real and not real' aspect of the shooting raises the question Mary had just consciously voiced. Perhaps the little child Mary wanted a special relationship with her father, excluding mother; a normal Oedipal situation. However if this wish was to some extent gratified, rather than given up as in an Oedipal resolution, the little Mary would feel very powerful, and guilty, and in fear of vengeful retaliation by the excluded mother.

Referring back to the story of Oedipus Rex, Oedipus feels terrible guilt when he realises that he has committed an actual crime; he can no longer deny the implications of his actions to himself. In Mary's case, her parents' divorce seemed to confirm to her that her phantasy had become reality; she could separate her parents. The delineation between phantasy and reality became blurred, she was overwhelmed by guilt at her 'crime' and she passed out, became unconscious, just as Oedipus blinded himself.

Britton (1992) writes the following, quoting from Freud's letters to Fliess concerning the Oedipus complex:

> ... he (Freud) conjured up a universal audience for the Greek drama of Oedipus Rex, in which 'Each member was once, in germ and in phantasy, just such an Oedipus.' Freud refers to the horror generated in the audience by 'the dream fulfilment here transplanted into reality' ... the horror, that is, of

Oedipus killing his father and marrying his mother, leading Jocasta his mother to suicide and Oedipus to blinding himself.

Resolution of Oedipal conflict rests upon an increased capacity to tolerate reality in terms of acceptance of the parents as the pro-creative couple, and a sexual identification usually with the parent of the same sex, which enables one to form a procreative relation-ship oneself.

Mary went on to tell me about her continuing intense jealousy of her sister (mother's favourite) who is happily married with a child. She followed this with an account of her own disastrous relationships of recent years. This suggested that she feels that her sister has been able to identify with the mother, to become a wife and mother herself, whereas Mary is unable to do so.

Mary's fear of a further breakdown became a predominant theme in the early phase of her therapy. Her omnipotent phantasies at times overwhelmed her sense of reality, which at such times 'got lost'. This was evidenced in memory loss, and Mary would turn up for sessions at the wrong time, on the wrong day.

In one session at this time Mary related a long story about her brother, who had been seriously injured in a car accident. Just before this event she had dreamed that her father had been shot; she had run to pick up his body, and was pervaded by a sense of bliss, of holiness. In Mary's mind, the dream and the actual event became fused. She told me in an anguished way that she should have pre-vented the accident by letting her brother know that he was in danger, immediately following the dream.

Here, Mary ignores differences between dreams and reality. It is of no consequence to her that the dream was about her father, not her brother. Phantasy and reality are undifferentiated. The dream of her father's death suggests pre-Oedipal longings to merge with the mother in blissful union yet this cannot be expressed in relation to the maternal object, even in dreams. Instead of a living mother there is a dead father.

Britton (1989), in *The Oedipus complex today*, draws on Klein's theory of the more primitive aspects of the Oedipus complex and

Bion's (1962) concept of 'container-contained'. He suggests that an early failure of maternal containment can severely hinder the child's capacity to perceive and to internalise the Oedipal triangular configuration. He explains this by the hypothesis that an infant must preserve, in his mind, a good maternal object in order to thrive. Failure to keep the feeding, life-giving mother as a good object would cause the infant to turn away from that upon which his survival depends. In Britton's view, in cases where the mother fails to provide adequate containment, the infant is impelled to split off and project the unmanageable and destructive feelings evoked in himself by the maternal failure to contain his emotional communications. These destructive feelings are projected into the third object in the Oedipal configuration, the father. In order to preserve the goodness of the feeding mother, the parental couple must not come together in the infant's mind or the mother would be contaminated by the dangerous father. Thus the Oedipal triangular configuration cannot be tolerated or allowed to exist in the infant's mind.

As Mary related to me her long account of her brother's accident and subsequent disability, her body was rigidly tense, her hands shaking, and a knot of tension stood out on her forehead. She seemed unreachable.

She concluded by raging against herself for allowing the accident to happen, and any interpretations I made seemed quite redundant. Suddenly she stopped mid-flow and said 'Why am I telling you this? It's not the point. I feel very far away. Can you tell by my eyes?'

At this moment Mary suddenly became aware of the two of us, separate people, in the room together, and the possibility of therapeutic containment; that I would be able to look into her eyes and perceive how she was feeling.

It was then possible to talk with Mary about her omnipotent way of functioning; her phantasy that she can cause her parents to divorce and know in advance that her brother was to have an accident. This mode of functioning rests upon denial of reality and can be psychotic when extreme.

In 1924 Freud (1924/1961n) wrote:

> ... one of the features which differentiate a neurosis from a psychosis is the fact that in a neurosis the ego, in its dependence on reality, suppresses a piece of the id (of instinctual life), whereas in a psychosis, this same ego, in the service of the id, withdraws from a piece of reality.

Relating this to the Oedipus complex, Klein (1926/1981a) wrote:

> At a very early age children become acquainted with reality through the deprivations it imposes on them. They defend themselves against reality by repudiating it. The fundamental thing, however, and the criterion of all later capacity for adaptation to reality is the degree in which they are able to tolerate the deprivations that result from the Oedipal situation.

Following Britton's (1989) argument that failure of maternal containment underlies an inability to adapt to the reality of the Oedipal situation, Mary seemed to be beginning to conceive of an object in the maternal transference who may be able to tell from her eyes that she is far away and desperately in need of containment.

The task that lay ahead was to find a way to help Mary to allow herself to be in touch with the intimacy of the reality of a two-person relationship; the closeness between therapist and patient, mother and baby, initially at a primitive, preverbal eye-to-eye level of contact. Only if this could be established, externally and internally, could Oedipal three-person issues be addressed.

Mary's hope that I would be able to tell from her eyes how far away she felt and bring her back into relationship with me, suggests a longing for closeness and understanding, but one that implies the separateness of two people; the distance necessary for communication, even at a primitive level. This would provide a basis for processes of introjective identification, and the possibility of establishing a good internal object.

Her bodily tension also had a primitive infantile quality, and evoked in me an urge similar to that which one may feel towards a tiny baby who needs physically holding and soothing. This of course could not be enacted, but was verbalised in interpretations.

After a few months of therapy, Mary said that she was feeling better, and indeed she seemed much less tense. The tight knot on her forehead had disappeared and she no longer shook as she spoke. She expressed gratitude for my help and said that she wanted to continue with the sessions; she had not expected to be understood.

She then went on to talk about a very exciting book she was reading, and immediately the feeling of closeness vanished. She told me that the book was about esoteric Eastern philosophy and that she had stayed awake all night when she had finished reading it. She said that it was about the transformation of sexual energy into higher energy by meditation, and this is why she feels so good today. Mary now seemed very 'high', she patted at her chest and said that she felt breathless and dizzy.

I felt that she had been frightened by a brief feeling of closeness to me when she expressed gratitude. Envy of the feeding mother-therapist may have been a factor in her sudden flight, yet fear was more in evidence in my counter-transference. I think that Mary may have approached the notion of a parental couple when she allowed herself to acknowledge me as someone who had helped her, separate from her, someone who may have a partner. Her choice of book seemed to confirm this idea: a one-person model of sexuality is safe, obviating the idea of the parental sexual couple. Mary's moments of closeness to me perhaps become suffused with sexuality, and are experienced as dangerous. She has to take flight, become 'high' and far-away again.

In order to understand why it felt so dangerous to Mary to allow herself to have an experience of containment in the therapeutic relationship, the question of guilt needs to be explored. Klein's (1935/1981d,1940/1981e) concept of the depressive position is relevant here, as it refers to the guilt, concern, and reparative impulses experienced in relation to the mother, arising out of the awareness that the mother who is attacked in phantasy for, amongst other things, excluding the child from parental intercourse, is the same mother who is loved and needed and upon whom the child depends for existence. In Klein's view these processes begin in the first year of life.

In the classical Freudian view the Oedipus complex is at its height at 3 to 4 years of age, but Kleinian theory locates precursors of the Oedipal configuration in infancy (Klein, 1926/1981a, 1928/1981b, 1945/1981f). Thus in the Kleinian view, simultaneous processes take place in the earliest years of childhood; the working through of depressive and Oedipal anxieties must take place if development is to proceed normally.

As Mary's therapy progressed she began to become deeply upset about the sessions she 'forgot' to attend, berating herself severely when she telephoned to apologise. Her attendance became regular, her demeanour calmer, and she began to work hard in her sessions, giving serious thought to the implications of her 'flights' from therapy in the form of both missed sessions and attacks on the contact between us (as in the example with the book, given above).

It seemed that Mary felt that I could withstand her attacks in a nonretaliatory way, unlike the vengeful mother of her internal world who had appeared in her dreams and phantasies. She began to take more care of herself, both of her health and her appearance. As she began to allow herself to feel helped in the therapy, so she began to be able to look after herself, identifying with a caring maternal object.

She formed a relationship with a man, very cautiously at first. Then followed a turbulent phase, with Mary unsure of her capacity to commit herself to a serious involvement, but after some months they had become a loving couple. This coincided with the ending of Mary's therapy, earlier than would have been optimal for external reasons, but Mary had made good use of weekly psychotherapy for nearly a year.

CONCLUSION

In this lecture I have discussed the psychic tasks that emerge at the transition from adolescence to adulthood. These tasks may be renegotiated as they arise in varying forms throughout the life-cycle, from infancy to old age, allowing renewed opportunities for further growth and development of the personality. The Oedipus complex may re-emerge as an unresolved conflict and give rise to a range of emotional difficulties from mild to severe, as young people face the task of finding an authentic adult identity for themselves.

Chapter 9

The transition from late adolescence to young adulthood: Student life

David Hardie

THE CHANGING ENVIRONMENT OF FURTHER AND HIGHER EDUCATION AND HOW THIS IMPINGES ON THE INDIVIDUAL STUDENT

Winnicott (1965) has eloquently described in his writings how the individual needs a 'facilitating environment' if he or she is to grow towards emotional and cognitive health. He shows how development is an interaction between the uniqueness of the individual inheritance and the environment that holds and contains the individual. Bion (1962) wrote in detail about the nature of a facilitating environment, in which he suggested that the infant needs mental and physical breast milk, the milk of understanding, that can transform fear and terror into something safer, as well as the physical milk that comforts and nourishes the physical organism— a breast that is both psyche and soma. If a mother, for instance, is chronically depressed (without the milk of understanding) following the birth of her baby and there is not a 'good enough' experience of physical and emotional holding and nurturing available from some other close figure, such as father or another relative, friend, or professional, then babies and young children may not thrive or develop satisfactorily. It is not, however, a one-way traffic, for lively and good-humoured babies frequently can coax and encourage their mothers to take an interest in them, and can help a mother gather herself.

There are many ways in which the environment can fail to provide what Bowlby (1998) called a 'secure base' for children, so that they grow up anxious and preoccupied with a fear of the unknown, a fear of falling apart, a fear of present and future betrayals. In the Robertsons' (1969) films about *Young children in brief separation* this was illustrated clearly and painfully. The expanding field of attachment research also confirms the importance of the nature of early relationships, and their sustaining impact on adult life. When as adults we have to meet challenging events such as major surgery, moving house, or loss of a loved person, we realise that our coping ability is precarious. Unable to use the defence of denial, we can become tense and anxious, and lose our sense of stablity.

In college or university, the manner of selection and the nature of the induction stage can affect the student's overall experience. The way new attachments are made have implications for that student's whole experience. Thought and time given to the process of 'settling in' may significantly affect drop-out rates. The process of detachment also needs understanding and attention. In a 3-year course the transition out into the wider world begins in earnest in the second year, when students become aware of the reality of the ending of their course. Psychologically, it is felt suddenly to be downhill, and typically the experience speeds up, culminating in the rituals of final assessment and graduation. The management of attachment and loss, those fundamental and creative emotional tasks, are at the heart of the learning experience. How each person manages these affects the quality of his or her emotional and academic experience of learning in further education. Sometimes this is brought home clearly and sadly when a student comes to college and does not have the emotional resources to attach at that point, and has to deal with extreme panic by sinking back into the more restricted world of their family home. Some concerned institutions are sensitive to these emotional aspects of learning and make good provision. The importance and power of holding individual students in mind and being aware of their emotional and academic needs cannot be emphasised enough if one wants to create a good learning environment.

Further education in the UK has changed dramatically in the last 10 years. Rapid and radical new structures have been forcefully imposed during a period of recession, shrinking GNP, and reduced central government funding. On the one hand this has been billed positively as an extensive democratisation of higher education, allowing far greater numbers access to post A level courses. On the other hand it has led to far larger teaching groups, less contact with teaching staff, and a greater reliance on computer learning. Lecturers, who are mostly untrained as teachers, have been overwhelmed by student demands and struggle to provide standards of academic teaching and pastoral care. Inevitably, in certain quarters, there has been a move away from a belief in the importance of human contact in learning. It is difficult for lecturers to remain concerned with individuals when they are subject themselves to deprivation and anxiety. Security of tenure for lecturers has been reduced, short-term or temporary contracts are the norm, and the profession is moving towards a division between lower-paid teachers and those employed to do research. This is mirrored in the emergence of premier league and second league universities. Sickness in the profession has risen as an indicator of increased stress.

The Flowers Report (Department of Education and Employment, 1993) ushered in rule by the accountants. Whereas this was welcome in certain ways to provide greater economic efficiency, the extremes of that way of thinking have at times led to peculiar blindness, such as when the idea of utilising educational space throughout the year led to exams being set at weekends, which offended some religious groups who staged a protest. The idea was quietly dropped. The bottom line is that 'open access' needs good support systems otherwise many students are disappointed and damaged and some will drop out.

At the same time as this expansion, there has been a rapid shift from full grants to a loan system topped up by a much reduced and less widely available grant, which is rapidly being phased out, which can leave students with debts by the end of a 3-year course. The student loan system often does not provide enough for students to maintain themselves adequately on their courses. The Dering Report (Department of Education and Employment, 1998) has recommended that students bear the higher costs of education and particularly that they should pay towards fees if their parents' joint income is above a certain figure. This new system involves a radical shift of financial responsibility onto the student and will have an effect on recruitment. Whether this effect will be short-term in duration no one can predict. What can be said is that in general students are now shouldering large long-term debts at the start of their adult lives and this, whatever the gloss put on it, will deter many potentially able students from embarking on further study. The new arrangements cast dark shadows over the start of young adults' lives. Student poverty has become a very real issue as noted by Cronin (1995), a Senior Student Advisor:

> What we have found in the Counselling and Advisory Service with students who come in financial hardship, is that expending the amount of energy that is required to juggle money around, repeatedly move home because of rent arrears and to work on low pay and long hours, seriously jeopardises their ability to concentrate on their academic work. Students in financial hardship are more concerned about 'survival'. This can cause illness, depression, poor health, bad diet, missed lectures and failed deadlines. They are working in order to survive rather than to earn some extra cash and there can be a constant balancing act between work and course work which can seriously affect their performance on their course.
>
> Most students who have accumulated debt want to hide it. They feel ashamed and some are very humiliated at having to beg. We frequently experience this with students applying to Access and Hardship funds. Often we suggest that they let their tutor know, but many are unwilling to do so, even though it is affecting their work. Mature students in particular express this difficulty.
>
> Some students have been forced into criminal acts to survive. Fare dodging, fraudulent claims for social security benefits and stealing are not uncommon and even prostitution has been known.

The degree of insecurity for both staff and students in most institutions has led to a lack of containment, which has affected the quality of the student experience. In the last 5 years there has been a considerable growth in depression, anxiety, and dysfunctional stress amongst students. This is not healthy for any individual and it is certainly not conducive to thoughtful study.

THE TRANSITION FROM LATE ADOLESCENCE TO YOUNG ADULTHOOD: THE STUDENT EXPERIENCE

Going to college or university is not a two-dimensional experience of studying a subject to get the tools to succeed in the wider adult world, it is a three-dimensional experience that involves passionate hopes and disturbing fears. There are idealistic hopes of a new, inspiring, better life. Ideas of being a more responsible person are laced with magical thinking such as: 'When I go to college I'll learn to cook' or 'When I go to college I'll keep my room tidy, I'll learn to do this and that'. The resolutions cry out healthily from the coming generation, as if the only thing stopping them doing these basic activities is their parents.

The major factor in the transition from late adolescence to young adulthood is the extent of the shift from a dependent reliance on external parental figures to a reliance on oneself and one's own internal figures that bear resemblance to, but are also different from, the real parents. One has to become, to a much greater extent, one's own parent while still retaining contact with helpful external adult figures. Although this process of differentiation, separation, and individuation has been going on since birth, the suddenness and the extreme nature of the shift in late adolescence and young adulthood destabilises everyone to some extent and destabilises many people in a very disturbing way. Often the different parts of the self are split extremely, seeming not to hang together, but have to live in separated compartments or other people are forced to look after them temporarily. It is a period that operates like a crucible in a blacksmith's shop, where extremes of feeling and thought are forged into new shapes. The ideal and the reality are creatively and disturbingly juxtaposed.

The work of the late adolescent brings these contradictions together. The move towards greater maturity and integration, hard and disturbing emotional work, involves a lot of adjustment by the honest part of the adolescent self. Adolescent growth can be hugely embarrassing, involving the giving up of passionately held attitudes. It is important that adults are tactful, a difficult position when they may also have to absorb that adolescent's anxiety, resentment, and aggression. The central concern of late adolescence is the reappraisal of relationships with the external and internal parents. Many students who come for help come because these unresolved relationships are hindering their growth to adulthood and their capacity as students to learn, study, face assessment, and sit exams.

Sometimes adolescents break down; sometimes very tragically they attempt suicide as a way of solving the burden of this particular journey (Laufer, 1995). Some young people have enough resources to relish the conflicts as adventures and their curiosity is stimulated by the experience. For most young people these years are at least a very mixed experience.

The central tasks of late adolescence are: (1) the separation from parents and the building of a more autonomous identity; (2) the establishment of an adult sexual identity, and the capacity to manage the conflicts between love and hate in an intimate relationship with someone of one's own generation; and (3) the development of a capacity for work, as well as the beginnings of a sense of direction towards employment or career. Some people have these tasks well organised by the end of their late adolescence, some take longer, and others never resolve these issues. Perhaps in a deep sense, most people only resolve some of these issues to an extent and spend the rest of their lives deepening their understanding and practice in these areas. Many people, often the highly creative, get stuck with one bit or another and very sensibly seek help through counselling or therapy. Some people teeter agonisingly on the brink of asking for proper help and end up in danger of leaving it too late to salvage much from their twenties, apart from endless repetitive circular experiments. It is hoped that for some, new attempts at understanding may be available as the pressure of time passing offers its powerful and objective interpretations to those who can bear to listen.

For the student, the educational environment operates in one sense as a transitional, protected space in between the greater dependence on parents of earlier adolescence and the harder and less sympathetic adult world of work and independent living. It is, in a way, a miniature society, with the Students' Union, the clubs, support services, medical and counselling services, advice about housing or accommodation, and careers advice all available within the institution.

Lecturers and teachers often evoke a parental kind of transference for learners of all ages. They are symbolically paternal figures who have authority and powers of assessment, and at the same time they may be experienced as maternal, nourishing figures who are offering knowledge to be taken in and digested. But they are not parents and therefore offer a new and less fraught arena in which to explore and experiment, where often intense idealisation and inspiration, so essential in learning, can be safely achieved.

The peer group is important for students as it is for all adolescents. It is a place for young people to work out their ideas, values, and relationships. Sometimes the group, which is usually a benign alternative space to relationships with parents and other older adults, can turn into a dangerous gang culture where anti-authority and anti-social values thrive in an extreme way. Copley (1993) comments on the peer group, and notes that:

> These groups provide conjoint playground cum workshops concerned with identity where young people can find out, in conjunction with others, what it is like to be this changing version of themselves: what interests them; whom they get on with, and why; how they experience.

Erikson (1950) talks of the need for the late adolescent to have space for a 'psychological moratorium', where these adjustments to becoming adult can take place. Time tends suddenly to speed up for young people, who are forced to be more in touch with a fuller version of reality. They often say that they are feeling old and the 'brave new world' is cracking in their minds as it turns into a frightening and heavy world of responsibility. Phobic symptoms such as panic attacks, agoraphobia, and claustrophobia may be experienced. The psychedelic quality of excitement and hope can rapidly turn into the monochromatic depression of an eternal life of grey 'nine-to-five-ness'. Winnicott is particularly sensitive to and in tune with the pain and pressures of late adolescence. He writes (Winnicott, 1971) of the infant's need for illusion:

> There is no possibility whatever for an infant to proceed from the pleasure principle to the reality principle or towards and beyond primary identification, unless there is a good enough mother. The good enough 'mother' (not necessarily the infant's own mother) is one who makes active adaptation to the infant's needs, an active adaptation that gradually lessens, according to the infant's growing ability to account for failure of adaptation and to tolerate frustration.

These are wise thoughts that all good and sensitive teachers and lecturers instinctively understand, whatever the age of the students they are teaching. There is nothing more damaging for a person's capacity to learn from experience than a parent or teacher who aggressively pushes tasks onto an individual before they actually have the equipment to understand and perform those tasks. This can lead to chronic lack of self-esteem, to feeling stupid, to building up false defences to achieve pseudo-learning or sometimes to become a bully to make other people feel stupid and frightened. To feel stupid is to feel the self annihilated.

In his essay *Contemporary concepts of adolescent development and their implications for higher education*, Winnicott (1968) argues passionately for adolescents to be allowed to be adolescents and for adults to engage with them without giving in falsely to their demands:

> Immaturity is a precious part of the adolescent scene. In this is contained the most exciting features of creative thought, new and fresh feeling, ideas for new living. Society needs to be shaken by the aspirations of those who are not responsible. If the adults abdicate, the adolescent becomes prematurely and by false process, adult. Advice to society could be: for the sake of adolescents and of their immaturity, do not allow them to step up and attain a false maturity by handing over to them responsibility that is not yet theirs, even though they may fight for it.

LATE ADOLESCENT IMPASSE AND THE ROLE OF PSYCHOANALYTIC THERAPY OR COUNSELLING IN ITS RESOLUTION

Four individual situations illustrate in a specific way some of the general issues I have sketched out.

Early Oedipal disappointment: clinical example

Joan, a 21-year-old music student, came for help with her depression. She had had a breakdown ending in an attempted suicide by overdose. She told me that she had lost her passion for her principal instrument and was thinking of giving up college although she was obviously a highly gifted musician. She began to tell me that what had led to the depression was her increased disturbance at a repeated pattern of older men falling in love with her, usually men she was involved with in a learning capacity. They were all situations involving men in authority who were in a supportive role towards her and the collapse of these relationships left her full of despair and guilt. She felt she may have had some part in this process but was really very unclear about what was going on. She told me with some embarrassment that they all remarked on her powerful, beautiful eyes. She was an attractive young woman with at times rather wide open, almost staring, slightly hypnotic eyes, that were vulnerable to or encouraged intrusion.

When we began to look into her past, she told a story of having been her father's favourite. She had one younger brother. She remembered at the age of 4, that as a country doctor he would take her by the hand on his rounds and how she enjoyed his rather exciting attention. At that point he literally, as she put it, disappeared. She found out later that he had had an affair with one of his female patients and had left the family home and gone to live with her. Since then Joan had only had infrequent, highly charged contacts with him. Her mother never wanted her to see him again and indeed, after the separation, mother became unwell and my client developed a rather guilty, over-concerned bond with her. When she left home to come to college her guilt became worse. She came for help in her first year suffering from acute depression.

I got the impression that this father in reality had had little capacity to manage his sexual and emotional boundaries and had been too close and adoring of his daughter whom he suddenly abandoned, leaving her traumatised in the middle of unresolved Oedipal longings. She began slowly to let me know that in her relationships with older men she somehow attracted them deeply into herself, they literally 'fell into love with her through her eyes' in a very intense kind of way. The results were disastrous for they tended to be teachers in authority, people who were married with children, people who needed to manage their contact with students with care. She began to let me know how at times she could be extremely controlling and cruel in these relationships and play with them rather like a cat with a mouse. She also told me how frightened she was about coming for therapy, because she feared that she might find out that she was evil, as her mother had often said she was.

While the reconstruction of the past made more and more sense about what had been going on in her life, it did not, on its own, help her to resolve these unconscious conflicts. But her relationship to me as a psychotherapist and an older man had many echoes to that of the relationship to her father, and indeed the same dynamic emerged with me. I think that the experience of having a safe situation, where these feelings could be explored without them being acted out by me or her, helped her to begin to feel differently and to recognise her fixation and addiction to something that was very destructive for all aspects of her growth. For the first time she found a boyfriend of her own age and began to explore her sexuality, which in reality had been very inhibited. She began to feel less anxious about abandonment. Older men became slowly less attractive to her and she became much more adept at spotting her own behaviour in these kind of relationships. She began to feel less depressed and to enjoy playing her instrument again. In relation to her mother, she became less guilty and more separated as, somewhere, I think she had felt that she had caused her father's disappearance and her mother's loss. She also contacted her father and began to be able to have a more realistic contact with him, neither too angry nor too idealising. She gave up her wishes to leave college.

In this work one can see how the unresolved aspects of her parental relationships from the past affected her internally so that her feelings about the traumatic abandonment of her childhood began to get acted out in her adult relationships in a way that particularly affected her capacity to work as a student and indeed threatened at one point her very existence. The therapy allowed the very strong positive qualities in her to mobilise themselves in a working alliance with me so that internal change could come about. If work can be done with people at this age before they become more chronically depressed, then good results can follow.

The effects of early deprivation on the learning relationship: clinical example

Maria, 18, was studying to be a nursery nurse and from the first meeting her teacher was made aware of her by how she communicated her presence, by the way she sat, giving off a scornful expression. The teacher discovered later that her parents had divorced when she was very young and her mother had been very depressed after her birth. During her first tutorial she disclosed to the teacher that before coming to college she had attempted suicide by cutting herself; this disturbed the teacher considerably. Maria's written skills were weak and although given extra support she found the assignments hard going. The relationship with the teacher began to change from abuse to idealisation, and she became overattached. It became clear that what she wanted was an enormous amount of personal attention, far beyond what could be given in the college setting. It seems that the lack of parental attention that Maria had received, led to her trying to get these needs met very concretely through the teacher and the college. This is a common situation where someone tries to get the institution quite concretely to be a new and ideal family. The educational institution is then pushed to be a kind of therapeutic community. Teachers should be concerned about the pastoral side of their job if only because student distress impinges so directly onto the learning situation, but there are limits to what an individual teacher or institution can provide. Maria needed her basic emotional needs as a person attended to before she could succeed in academic study. Her choice of training to be a nursery nurse was possibly partly to do with her own inner child's wish to be given attention. The teacher tried over time to refer her for counselling but the feelings of rejection and pain of losing the special attention from her teacher made it impossible for Maria to seek help elsewhere. In the end she failed her assignments and had to leave, much to the teacher's distress and dismay.

The capacity to learn through studying involves taking things in at a deep level and it originates from and is linked to the early experiences of taking in nourishment physically and emotionally.

Our language is full of the language of this overlap and people talk of 'food for thought' and 'taking in knowledge' and after a binge of revision students will say that they feel 'stuffed full of facts'. Many learning difficulties are actually a kind of eating disorder, involving problems of taking in and digesting (Williams, 1997). When people have finished essays or dissertations they often talk with pleasure of the relief of having got rid of something (excretion) and sometimes they will talk of having given birth if they feel that they have achieved something creative. There are primitive unconscious links between learning and feeding, eating, digestion, evacuation, and also sex, conception, and birth.

The Emperor's clothes—false potency in a young adult man: clinical example

John, 18, was was very reluctant to come to counselling. He was the oldest child in the family. His parents had separated when he was 6. He admitted in a nonchalant way that he was stressed out all the time and was unable to concentrate, which made his studying at college and his work experience impossible for him. He always ended up absenting himself from both. He also acknowledged that he had frequent very explosive rows with his mother. But in his mind there was a mystery surrounding his problems; he couldn't make head or tail of it. His life in reality seemed to be going nowhere and he had serious blocks to learning. His attendance at the counselling was sporadic and there was a strong sense of him trying to avoid his reality. Bit by bit a picture emerged. John, from the age of 12, encouraged by his mother, seemed to have taken his father's place when he left and with a mixture of resentment and secret enjoyment of this powerful role, he had tried to instil some order and discipline into what sounded like a rather chaotic family life. His mother sounded quite weak and left John to organise things, but she would also undermine him. As he became literally a grown man the tension between him and his mother became worse and the rows ensued. The implicit sexuality in this relationship came more dangerously to the fore in John's adolescence and was partially expressed, partially deflected by these rages. In the counselling, he told of how outside the home he kept failing badly at everything he tried and what became clear was that whenever he came up against a real authority he had a panic attack. He was terrified of exams and tests and could not concentrate or take anything in as he was so anxious about failing. Slowly, against enormous resistance and fighting the authority of the counsellor to see things clearly, he began to acknowledge that underneath his enjoyment of being 'father' of the house, he felt like the Emperor without any clothes, a little boy who had put on father's clothes without having been able to become a grown up the real way, i.e. slowly and painfully, by learning through experience with parental help. He was terrified of being found out by a real 'father' kind of person. As Winnicott would say, he had not been given the chance to be immature; the adults had allowed him to have a false authority when he should have been able to be an adolescent.

The slowness of the counselling work underlies just how attractive, almost addictive, this stolen authority was and how hard it was for the healthy, more realistic part of him to push for something safer and with better foundations. It was made more difficult because his mother was colluding at an emotional level in some kind of phantasy of her son being her husband, so that there was an unconscious incestuous *folie à deux* in operation. Until this was begun to be given up and the feelings of loss in relation to his father experienced, there was no way that the slow journey of learning from immaturity to maturity could take place, a hard road to tread at 18. For people in John's psychological situation, achievements in personal relationships and in studying will continually be sabotaged unless this work on the foundations of the personality are done.

Exam anxiety—the process of assessment

Exams and assessments are unavoidable for students, and can evoke strong, often primitive emotions. These feelings go back to very early in life and are about fears concerned with survival, whether people are going to be killed, whether they are lovable, whether sibling jealousy will strike one down if one really allows oneself to be successful and, in phantasy, the most desirable child in the department. There seems to be an escalating level of anxiety for people doing further degrees, such as PhDs. There is always heightened anxiety surrounding exams as they are the key to the door that leads on to the future and to adult responsibilities. They arouse very mixed feelings in people as the key to passing or failing the test after it has been written is firmly in the hands of the internal and external examiners. The role of the external examiner is to ensure that the pressures on teachers inside do not disturb their objective analysis. The following clinical example shows what may be stirred up by exams.

Clinical example

Hassan was in the middle of his PhD when he came for help as he was slowing down, getting stuck, and was having to use most of his energy getting down to work and trying to keep himself from falling asleep. As he approached the finishing of the PhD he was clearly suffering from severe anxiety and resistance to the work. His parents had both been lecturers but not in universities, and they had immense ambitions for him to get to the top of the tree. Cognitive and educational achievement had been the thing from day one, and as a child he was severely restricted from going out to play as they kept his nose to the grindstone in what seemed to have been a rather cruel and obsessional way, although well meant. He said himself that he felt he had never been given warmth or love, and praise only came occasionally when he did well at school; he felt those moments were the nearest to love that he had experienced from his parents. It was a very sad picture and he cried about it and got in touch with real resentment and anger with his parents, which over some time he began to tell them about. His unconscious problem was a difficult one, for to finish the PhD would be to fulfil his parents' wishes and to somehow acknowledge that what they had given him was good enough, which in truth he did not feel. It would also secure for him a permanent full-time university post, not something that grows on every tree these days. Somewhere he equated failing the PhD with getting back at or through to his parents about the seriousness of his emotional state and how strongly he felt about his deprivation. But he also knew that failing the PhD would be shooting himself in the foot and really making himself a failure. The difficulty for him was in coming to terms with having missed out on a great deal in his childhood so that he could make the best of what he did have and perhaps look for some of what he had missed in his adult relationships. It was like pushing a very heavy boulder up a very steep hill and as he slowly got nearer to the end it became more dangerous. One night he crashed his car through lack of concentration. He became more and more exhausted and disorientated and it seemed he might finally break down completely. In the end somehow he managed to face the ending of it with all the fears of parental rejection if he failed. The actual parents and the examiners became fused in his mind because for him the love he did get was expressed through his successful work at school and failure was expressed by their anger and rejection.

Although he passed his PhD, predictably this did not resolve Hassan's internal conflicts. After a short time he became extremely depressed, which was accompanied by severe self-loathing and self-deprecation. Temporarily he sensibly accepted some medication for his depression from his GP. Meanwhile, Hassan had to decide whether or not to have much more intensive and containing psychotherapy, which would give him a chance to resolve his problems. So often the gaining of a degree is idealised and seen as a way of resolving serious internal conflict. It never does, although it may give satisfaction and help towards employment, which is different.

Sudden change and transition

Davar (1996) addresses issues involving abrupt change and transition in his paper *Surviving or living? A question of containment.* He looks at the effects on individuals of abrupt and sudden change. He talks about the process and the qualities needed to adjust to change and grow from it, rather than just survive it. He also looks at the effects on the personality when the stress of change cannot be contained and managed. He describes two individuals who break down and then comments:

> In this series of events there is a rupture in the environmental containment and its impact was to make the individual anxiety levels unmanageable and unbearable. I believe they both had

an experience in which there was no adequate 'social container', which I think is a useful term to describe a failure of a significant environmental response that could absorb an individual's anxieties. As a result of this lack both these people developed anxieties of such a pitch that they could not manage to contain their conflicts by themselves and this led to a gesture of suicide as an appeal for help and containment.

The implications of this example are very clear. As the social containers shrink so does the arena for projection and containment, and the pressure on the individual to contain anxieties and conflict increases. So the more the individual is going to have to provide his or her containment independent of a supporting network. The more absent the container, the more likelihood of spillage of anxiety, using a simple hydraulic method.

He concludes his comments about refugees or anyone undergoing abrupt transition and change:

> So, to summarise, I believe that a healthy re-adaptation will depend primarily on the internal resources of the refugee and secondarily on the social networks which support the refugee. If the refugee has a containing internal image this will help a great deal as will receptive containment. A combination of both factors is likely to ensure a good transition, but if one, or both, of these variables is missing this will lead to alienation and profound personal problems in the future.
>
> Davar 1996

I think that these formulations are very relevant to students going to college, as the transition from adolescence to young adulthood involves them in being emotional refugees for a period of time until they settle into their new state.

CONCLUSION

There are many factors that influence the learning situation for people entering higher education, both intrapsychic and organisational. The crucial factor for the individual is the question of internal emotional resources. But whether these can be fostered may also depend on whether educational organisations can support both staff and students and can create emotionally thoughtful environments. A young person's academic and social experience can determine whether he or she fails, drops out, or can fulfil his or her potential, thus providing a springboard for their future.

Endpiece

Debbie Hindle and Marta Vaciago Smith

Our journey ends at this point, but life is by no means at an end. We are leaving our subjects at the threshold of adulthood. The last lectures describe young adults within a specific organisation/ social context and point to the fact that we are not only influenced by our surrounding circumstances but are integrally part of them. More changes and transitions are to come. Each stage of development described in the book forms the template for future development.

Leaving home anticipates the possibility of forming new relationships, meeting partners, and eventually having children of one's own. Whether or not each of these functions is fulfilled, as a partner or a parent, a fuller involvement with the world marks the move into adulthood. Retreat or withdrawal from active participation through work, relationships, and creative endeavours will result in stunting of personality. Yet involving oneself with others, allowing one's own internal world to enter into contact with others' internal worlds, inevitably leads to confusion, tension, and conflict.

Throughout the lectures, the contributors have described the complex nature of the development of the personality and of interpersonal relationships. As we have seen illustrated in the various lectures, the dynamics between intimate family relationships and interaction with the wider world are ongoing. A further dynamic is a wish to be on one's own, hermit-like, against the turmoil of being involved.

The pull to extract ourselves from our families of origin, essentially to be oneself, is fundamental. Yet each of us carries within us the combined experiences of our family. It is this introjected experience that we bring to new relationships. Personality development can be seen as interchangeable with the sense of identity or individuality, but the book is a testimony to the basic need for relatedness. Diversity brought by relatedness generates what we have come to visualise as a rich pattern, like a mosaic, which leads to a deeper understanding of oneself and others. When originally given, the lectures were not intended to be fixed in book form, but to be a stimulus for further thought and discussion. Similarly, we hope that the readers have felt encouraged to link the lectures with their personal experiences, as a child, a family member, and in relation to their work. As personality development remains an open-ended process, we hope this book generates food for thought and further reading.

References

Adamo, S. & Magagna, J. (1998). Oedipal anxieties, the birth of a second baby and the role of the observer. *The International Journal of Infant Observation, 1* (2).

Ainsworth, M. (1982). Attachment retrospect and prospect. In C. M. Parkes & J. Stevenson Hinde (Eds.), *The place of attachment in human behaviour.* New York: Basic Books.

Ainsworth, M., Blehar, M., Waters, E. & Wall, S. (1978). *Patterns of attachment: Assessed in the Strange Situation and at home.* Hillsdale, NJ: Lawrence Erlbaum.

Alvarez, A. (1989). Developments towards the latency period: Splitting and the need to forget in borderline children. *Journal of Child Psychotherapy, 15* (2).

Alvarez, A. (1992). *Live company.* London: Routledge.

Andric, I. (1959). *The bridge over the Drina.* London: George Allen & Unwin.

Baruch, G. (1997). The process of engaging disturbance in psychoanalytic psychotherapy: Patterns of practice. *Bulletin of the Menninger Clinic, 61* (3).

Bick, E. (1968). The experience of skin in early object relations. *International Journal of Psycho-Analysis, 49* (2).

Bick, E. (1986). Further considerations on the function of the skin in early object relations. *British Journal of Psychotherapy, 2* (4).

Bion, W. R. (1967b). The differentiation of the psychotic from the non-sychotic personalities. In *Second thoughts: Selected papers in psychoanalysis.* London: Heinemann. (Original work published 1957.)

Bion, W. R. (1961). *Experiences in groups.* London: Tavistock Publications.

Bion, W. R. (1962). *Learning from experience.* London: Heinemann.

Bion, W. R. (1967a). *Second thoughts: Selected papers in psychoanalysis.* London: Heinemann.

Biran, H. (1997). Myths, memories and roles—how they live again in the group process. *Free Associations, 7* (Part 1, No. 41).

Bloch, H. S. (1995). *Adolescent development, psychopathology and treatment.* Madison, CT: International University Press.

Blos, P. (1962). *On adolescence.* New York: Free Press.

Bourne, S. & Lewis, E. (1992). *A psychological aspect of stillbirth and neonatal death: An annotated bibliography.* London: Tavistock Publications.

Bowlby, J. (1969). *Attachment and loss. Vol. 1: Attachment.* London: Hogarth Press.

Bowlby, J. (1973). *Attachment and loss. Vol. 2: Separation: Anxiety and anger.* London: Hogarth Press.

Bowlby, J. (1979a). *The making and breaking of affectional bonds.* London: Tavistock Publications.

Bowlby, J. (1979b). On knowing what you are not supposed to know and feeling what you are not supposed to feel. *Canadian Journal of Psychiatry, 24* (5).

Bowlby, J. (1988). *A secure base: Clinical applications of attachment theory.* London: Routledge.

Brazelton, B. T. & Cramer, B. G. (1991). *The earliest relationship: Parents, infants and the drama of early attachment.* London: Karnac.

Britton, R. (1983). Breakdown and reconstitution of the family circle. In M. Boston & R. Szur (Eds.), *Psychotherapy with severely deprived children.* London: Routledge & Kegan Paul.

Britton, R. (1989). The missing link: Parental sexuality in the Oedipus complex. In J. Steiner (Ed.), *The Oedipus complex today: Clinical implications.* London: Karnac.

Britton, R. (1992). The Oedipus situation and the depressive position. In R. Anderson (Ed.), *Clinical lectures on Klein and Bion.* London: Routledge.

Britton, R., Feldman, M. & O'Shaughnessy, E. (1989). *The Oedipus complex today: Clinical implications.* London: Karnac.

Cancrini, T. (1998). Precocious Oedipal fantasies and countertransference. *Journal of Child Psychotherapy, 24* (3).

Chamberlain, D. (1987). The cognitive newborn: A scientific update. *British Journal of Psychotherapy, 4* (1).

Chasseguet-Smirgel, J. (1985). *Creativity and perversion.* London: Free Association Books.

Coleridge, S. T. (1992) *The collected works of S. T. Coleridge.* Princeton, N.J.: Princeton University Press.

Copley, B. (1993). *The world of adolescence: Literature, society and psychoanalytic psychotherapy.* London: Free Association Books.

Cordess, C. & Williams, A. H. (1996). The criminal act and acting out. In C. Cordess and M. Cox (Eds.), *Forensic psychotherapy Vol. 1: Mainly theory.* London: Jessica Kinglsley.

Cronin, M. (1995). Poverty and containment. In A. Heyno (Ed.), *Managing poverty*, London: University of Westminster Press.

Dartington, A. (1994). The significance of the outsider in families and other social groups. In S. Box, B. Copley, J. Magagna and E. Moustaki Smilansky (Eds.), *Crisis at adolescence: Object relations therapy with the family*. London: Aronson.

Davar, E. (1996). Surviving or living? A question of containment. *Psychodynamic Counselling*, 2 (3).

Daws, D. (1996). *Post natal depression and the family: Conversations that go away*. Lecture given at the NCT National Conference (18.4.95) on 'Post natal depression: Focus on a neglected issue'.

Department of Education and Employment. (1993). *Higher Education Funding Council: Review of the academic year: A report of the Committee of Inquiry* (Chaired by Lord Flowers). School curriculum and assessment authority publications.

Department of Education and Employment. (1998). *Higher education for the 21st century: Response to the Dering Report*. School curriculum and assessment authority publications.

Deutsch, H. (1946). *The psychology of women: Psychoanalytic interpretation. Vol. 1: Girlhood*. London: Research Books.

Edwards, J. (1999). You can't miss something you never had. Can you? *Journal of Child Psychotherapy*, 5, (2).

Edwards, J. & Daws, D. (1996). Psychotherapy for school-refusing children with separation anxiety. In I. Berg and J. Nursten (eds.), *Unwillingly to school*. London: Gaskell.

Eliot, T. S. (1963). *Collected poems*. London: Faber & Faber.

Emde, R. (1994). Three roads intersecting: Changing viewpoints in the psychoanalytic story of Oedipus. In M. Ammanti & D. Stern (Eds.), *Psychoanalysis and development. Representations and narratives*. New York and London: New York University Press.

Erikson, E. (1950). *Childhood and society*. Harmondsworth, UK: Penguin.

Erikson, E. (1968). *Identity, youth and crisis*. New York: Norton & Co.

Ferenczi, S. (1909). Introjection and transference. In S. Ferenczi (Ed). *First contributions to psychoanalysis*. London: Hogarth Press.

Fonagy, P. & Moran, G. S. (1991). Understanding psychic change in child analysis. *International Journal of Psycho-Analysis*, 72 (1).

Fraiberg, S. (1980). *Clinical studies in infant mental health: The first year of life*. New York: Basic Books.

Freud, A. (1958). Adolescence. *Psychoanalytic study of the child No. 13*. New York: International University Press.

Freud, A. (1969). Adolescence as a developmental disturbance. In *The writings of Anna Freud, Vol. VII, 1966–1970*. New York: International University Press.

Freud, A. (1980). *Normality and pathology in childhood* (revised ed.). London: Hogarth Press.

Freud, S. (1961a). Extracts from the Fleiss papers. In J. Strachey (Ed. and Trans.), *The standard edition of the complete psychological works of Sigmund Freud* (Vol. 1). London: Hogarth Press. (Original work published 1897.)

Freud, S. (1961b). Sexuality in the aetiology of the neuroses. In J. Strachey (Ed. and Trans.), *The standard edition of the complete psychological works of Sigmund Freud* (Vol. 3). London: Hogarth Press. (Original work published 1898.)

Freud, S. (1961c). The interpretation of dreams. In J. Strachey (Ed. and Trans.), *The standard edition of the complete psychological works of Sigmund Freud* (Vol. 5). London: Hogarth Press. (Original work published 1899.)

Freud, S. (1961d). Three essays on the the theory of sexuality. In J. Strachey (Ed. and Trans.), *The standard edition of the complete psychological works of Sigmund Freud* (Vol. 7). London: Hogarth Press. (Original work published 1905.)

Freud, S. (1961e). Fragment of an analysis of a case of hysteria.' In J. Strachey (Ed. and Trans.), *The standard edition of the complete psychological works of Sigmund Freud* (Vol. 7). London: Hogarth Press. (Original work published 1905.)

Freud, S. (1961f). Analysis of a phobia in a five-year old boy. In J. Strachey (Ed. and Trans.), *The standard edition of the complete psychological works of Sigmund Freud* (Vol. 10). London: Hogarth Press. (Original work published 1909.)

Freud, S. (1961g). Formulations on the two principles of mental functioning. In J. Strachey (Ed. and Trans.), *The standard edition of the complete psychological works of Sigmund Freud* (Vol. 12). London: Hogarth Press. (Original work published 1911.)

Freud, S. (1961h). Totem and taboo. In J. Strachey (Ed. and Trans.), *The standard edition of the complete psychological works of Sigmund Freud* (Vol. 13). London: Hogarth Press. (Original work published 1913.)

Freud, S. (1961i). Mourning and melancholia. In J. Strachey (Ed. and Trans.), *The standard edition of the complete psychological works of Sigmund Freud* (Vol. 14). London: Hogarth Press. (Original work published 1917.)

Freud, S. (1961j). From the history of an infantile neurosis. In J. Strachey (Ed. and Trans.), *The standard edition of the complete psychological works of Sigmund Freud* (Vol. 18). London: Hogarth. (Original work published 1918.)

Freud, S. (1961k). Beyond the pleasure principle. In J. Strachey (Ed. and Trans.), *The standard edition of the complete psychological works of*

Sigmund Freud (Vol. 18). London: Hogarth Press. (Original work published 1920.)

Freud, S. (1961l). The ego and the id. In J. Strachey (Ed. and Trans.), *The standard edition of the complete psychological works of Sigmund Freud* (Vol. 19). London: Hogarth Press. (Original work published 1923.)

Freud, S. (1961m). The dissolution of the Oedipus complex. In J. Strachey (Ed. and Trans.), *The standard edition of the complete psychological works of Sigmund Freud* (Vol. 19). London: Hogarth Press. (Original work published 1924.)

Freud, S. (1961n). The loss of reality in neurosis and psychosis.' In J. Strachey (Ed. and Trans.), *The standard edition of the complete psychological works of Sigmund Freud* (Vol. 19). London: Hogarth Press. (Original work published 1924.)

Freud, S. (1961o). Inhibitions, symptoms and anxiety. In J. Strachey (Ed. and Trans.), *The standard edition of the complete psychological works of Sigmund Freud* (Vol. 20). London: Hogarth Press. (Original work published 1925.)

Freud, S. (1961p). Female sexuality. In J. Strachey (Ed. and Trans.), *The standard edition of the complete psychological works of Sigmund Freud* (Vol. 21). London: Hogarth Press. (Original work published 1931.)

Freud, S. (1961q). New introductory lectures on psychoanalysis. In J. Strachey (Ed. and Trans.), *The standard edition of the complete psychological works of Sigmund Freud* (Vol. 22). London: Hogarth Press. (Original work published 1933.)

Furman, E. (1994). Early aspects of mothering. *Journal of Child Psychotherapy, 20* (2).

Furniss, T. (1991). *The multi-professional handbook of sexual abuse.* London: Routledge.

Gaffney, B. & Reyes, P. (1999). Gender identity disorder. In M. Lanyado & A. Horne (Eds.). *The handbook of child and adolescent psychotherapy: Psychoanalytic approaches.* London: Routledge.

Gesell, A. (1988). *The embryology of behaviour: The beginnings of the human mind.* London: MacKeith Press. (Original work published 1945.)

Gorrell-Barnes, G., Thompson, P., Daniel, D. & Bierckardt, N. (1998). *Growing up in step families.* Oxford: Oxford Universtity Press.

Hering, C. (1997). Symbolisation and sublimation: Some thoughts on the vicissitudes of earliest passions. Unpublished paper given at a public lecture at the Institute of Psychoanalysis, London.

Hindle, D. (1998). Loss and delinquency: Two adolescents' experience of prison as an external container for psychic pain. *Journal of Child Psychotherapy, 24* (1).

Hinshelwood, R. D. (1991). *A dictionary of Kleinian thought.* London: Free Association Books.

Holloway, W. & Featherstone, B. (1997). *Mothering and ambivalence.* London: Routledge.

Holmes, J. (1993). *John Bowlby and Attachment Theory.* London: Routledge.

Klaus, M. & Kennell, J. (1982). *Maternal-infant bonding.* St. Louis, MO: Mosey.

Klein, M. (1961) *Narrative of a child analysis.* London: Hogarth Press.

Klein, M. (1975). Early stages of the Oedipal conflict. In *The psychoanalysis of children.* London: Hogarth Press. (Original work published 1927.)

Klein, M. (1980a). *The psychoanalysis of children* (rev.). London: Hogarth Press. (Original work published 1932.)

Klein, M. (1980b). The mutual influences in the development of the ego and the id. In *Envy and gratitude and other works.* London: Hogarth Press. (Original work published 1945.)

Klein, M. (1980c). Our adult world and its roots in infancy. In *Envy and gratitude and other works.* London: Hogarth Press. (Original work published 1958.)

Klein, M. (1981a). The psychological principles of early analysis. In *Love, guilt and reparation and other works.* London: Hogarth Press. (Original work published 1926.)

Klein, M. (1981b). Early stages of the Oedipus conflict. In *Love, guilt and reparation and other works.* London: Hogarth Press. (Original work published 1928.)

Klein, M. (1981c). The importance of symbol-formation in the development of the ego. In *Love, guilt and reparation and other works.* London: Hogarth Press. (Original work published 1930.)

Klein, M. (1981d). A contribution to the psychogenesis of manic-depressive states. In *Love, guilt and reparation and other works.* London: Hogarth Press. (Original work published 1935.)

Klein, M. (1981a). Mourning and its relation to manic-depressive states. In *Love, guilt and reparation and other works.* London: Hogarth Press. (Original work published 1940.)

Klein, M. (1981f). The Oedipus complex in the light of early anxieties. In *Love, guilt and reparation and other works.* London: Hogarth Press. (Original work published 1945.)

Kraemer, S. (1991). The origins of fatherhood: An ancient family process. *Family Process, 30* (4).

Laplanche, J. & Pontalis, J. B. (1973). *The language of psycho-analysis.* London: Hogarth Press.

Laufer, M. (1995). *The suicidal adolescent.* London: Karnac.

Laufer, M. & Laufer, M. E. (1984). *Adolescence and developmental breakdown.* London: Yale University Press.

Liley, H. W. (1972). The foetus as a personality. *Australian and New Zealand Journal of Psychiatry, 6.*

Lupinacci, I. (1998). Reflections on early stages of the Oedipus complex: The parental couple in relation to psychoanalytic work. *Journal of Child Psychotherapy 24* (3).

Masson, J. (1989). *Against therapy warning: Psychotherapy may be hazardous to your mental health.* London: Collins.

McFadyen, A. (1994). *Special care babies and their developing relationships.* London: Routledge.

Meltzer, D. (1973). *Sexual states of mind.* Strath Tay, UK: Clunie Press.

Miller, L. (1993). *Understanding your eight year old.* London: Rosendale Press.

Miller, L., Rustin, M. E., Rustin, M. J. & Shuttleworth, J. (1989). *Closely observed infants.* London: Duckworth.

Milne, A. A. (1928). *The house at Pooh Corner.* London: Methuen.

Money-Kyrle, R. E. (1978a). Cognitive development. In *The collected papers of Roger Money-Kyrle.* Strath Tay, UK: Clunie Press. (Original work published 1960.)

Money-Kyrle, R. E. (1978b). The aim of psychoanalysis (orig. 1968) In *The collected papers of Roger Money-Kyrle.* Strath Tay, UK: Clunie Press. (Original work published 1968.)

Negri, R. (1994). *The newborn in the intensive care unit: a neuropsychoanalytic prevention model.* London: Karnac.

Offer, D. & Offer, J. (1975). *From teenage to young manhood: a psychological study.* New York: Basic Books.

Ogden, T. (1989). *The primitive edge of experience.* London: Karnac.

O'Shaughnessy, E. (1964). The absent object. *Journal of Child Psychotherapy, 1* (2).

Parkes, C. M., Stevenson-Hinde, J. and Marris, P. (1991). *Attachment across the life cycle.* London and New York: Routledge.

Piaget, J. (1975). Intellectual development of the adolescent. In A. Esman (Ed.) *The psychology of adolescence: Essential readings.* New York: International Universities.

Pincus, L. & Dare, C. (1978). *Secrets in the family.* New York: Pantheon Books.

Piontelli, A. (1992). *From foetus to child: An observational and psychoanalytic study.* London: Routledge.

Raphael-Leff, J. (1993). *Pregnancy—the inside story.* London: Sheldon Press.

Reid, S. (Ed.). (1997). *Developments in infant observation: The Tavistock model.* London: Routledge.

Rey, H. (1994). *Universals of psychoanalysis in the treatment of psychotic and borderline states.* London: Free Association Books.

Robertson, J. & Robertson, J. (1969). *Young children in brief separation* [Film]. Ipswich, UK: Concord Films.

Robinson, M. (1997). *Divorce: A family transitio: When private sorrow becomes a public matter.* London: Karnac.

Salzberger-Wittenberg, I., Henry, G. & Osborne, E. (1983). *The emotional experience of teaching and learning.* London: Routledge.

Schaffer, H. R. (1996). *Social development.* Oxford: Blackwell.

Schave, D. & Schave, B. (1989). *Early adolescence and the search for self: A developmental perspective.* New York: Praeger.

Segal, H. (1978). On symbolism. *International Journal of Psycho-Analysis, 59* (2).

Segal, H. (1981). A psychoanalytical approach to aesthetics. In *The work of Hanna Segal.* London: Free Association Books.

Segal, H. (1989). Introduction. In R. Britton, M. Feldman & E. O'Shaughnessy, *The Oedipus complex today: Clinical implications.* London: Karnac.

Segal, H. (1991). *Dream, phantasy and art.* London: Routledge.

Stanton, M. (1994). Sigmund Freud's case. *The Tablet,* February 1994.

Steiner, J. (1985). Turning a blind eye: The cover-up for Oedipus. *International Review of Psycho-Analysis, 12* (5).

Steiner, J. (1993). *Psychic retreats.* London: Routledge.

Steiner, J. (1996). The aim of psychoanalysis in theory and practice. *International Journal of Psycho-Analysis, 77* (6).

Townsend, S. (1982). *The secret diary of Adrian Mole aged 13½.* London: Methuen.

Valman, H. B. & Pearson, J. F. (1980). What the foetus feels? *British Medical Journal, 280* (6209).

Williams, G. (1997). *Internal landscapes and foreign bodies: eating disorders and other pathologies.* London: Duckworth.

Williams, M. H. (Ed.). (1987). *Collected papers of Martha Harris and Esther Bick.* Strath Tay, UK: The Clunie Press.

Wingate, P. (Ed.) (1983) *Penguin Medical Encyclopedia.* Harmondsworth, UK: Penguin.

Winnicott, D. W. (1958). Birth memories, birth trauma and anxiety. In *Through paediatrics to psychoanalysis.* London: Hogarth Press. (Original work published 1949.)

Winnicott, D. W. (1964). *The child, the family and the outside world.* Harmondsworth, UK: Pelican.

Winnicott, D. W. (1964, May.) Youth will not sleep. *New Society,* May.

Winnicott, D. W. (1965). *The maturational processes and the facilitating environment.* London: Hogarth.

Winnicott, D. W. (1968). Contemporary concepts of adolescent development and their implications for higher education. Presented at a Symposium of the British Students' Health Association.

Winnicott, D. W. (1971). *Playing and reality*. London: Tavistock.

Winnicott, D. W. (1984). Struggling through the doldrums. In C. Winnicott & M. Davis (Eds.), *Deprivation and delinquency*. London: Tavistock Publications. (Original work published 1963.)

Winnicott, D. W. (1986). Adolescent immaturity. In C. Winnicott, R. Shepherd & M. Davis (Eds.), *Home is where we start from*. London: Penguin. (Original work published 1968.)

Selected reading list

Helpful dictionaries of psychoanalytic terms

Hinshelwood, R. D. (1992). *A dictionary of Kleinian thought* (2nd ed.). London: Free Association Press.
Laplanche, J. & Pontalis, J.-B. (1985). *The language of psycho-analysis.* London: Hogarth Press.

Relevant journals

Journal of Child Psychotherapy, published for the Association of Child Psychotherapists by Routledge, Rankine Road, Basingstoke, Hampshire RG24 8PR, UK.
The International Journal of Infant Observation and its Applications, published by the Tavistock Clinic Foundation in association with the Universities of East London Press: The Tavistock Centre, 120 Belsize Lane, London NW3 5BA, UK.

FURTHER SELECTED READING ON
Personality development

Harris, M. (1975). *Thinking about infants and young people.* Strath Tay, UK: Clunie Press.
Rayner, E. (1993). *Human development: An introduction to the psychodynamics of growth, maturity and ageing* (3rd rev. ed.). London: Routledge.
Schmit Neven, R. (1997). *Emotional milestones from birth to adulthood: A psychodynamic approach.* London: Jessica Kingsley.
Waddell, M. (1998). *Inside lives: Psychoanalysis and the growth of the personality.* London: Duckworth.

Development in a family context

Bowlby, J. (1979). *The making and breaking of affectional bonds.* London: Tavistock.

Brazelton, B. T. & Cramer, B. G. (1991). *The earliest relationship: Parents, infants and the drama of early attachment.* London: Karnac.

Clulow, C. F. (1982). *To have and to hold: The first baby and preparing couples for parenthood.* Aberdeen: Aberdeen University Press.

Dowling, E. & Osborne, E. (1985). *The family and school: A joint systems approach to problems with children* (2nd ed.). London: Routledge.

Gorrell-Barnes, G., Thompson. P., Daniel. D. & Burchardt, N. (1998). *Growing up in step families.* Oxford: Oxford University Press.

Klaus, M. and Kennel, J. (1982). *Maternal and infant bonding.* St Louis, MO: Mosey.

Kroll, B. (1996). *Chasing rainbows: Children, divorce and loss.* Lyme Regis: Russell House Publishing.

Raphael-Leff, J. (1991). *Psychological processes of childbearing.* London: Chapman Hall.

Raphael-Leff, J. (1993). *Pregnancy—the inside story.* London: Sheldon Press.

Robinson, M. (1997). *Divorce: A family transition: When private sorrow becomes a public matter.* London: Karnac.

Rustin, M. E. & Rustin, M. J. (1987). *Narratives of love and loss: Studies in modern children's fiction.* London: Verso.

Salzberger-Wittenberg, I., Henry, G. & Osborne, E. (1983). *The emotional experience of teaching and learning.* London: Routledge.

Sinason, V. (1992). *Mental handicap and the human condition.* London: Free Association Books

Skynner, A. C. R. & Cleese, J. (1984). *Families and how to survive them.* London: Methuen.

Winnicott, D. W. (1964). *The child, the family and the outside world.* Harmondsworth, UK: Penguin.

Winnicott, D. W. (1969). *Playing and reality.* Harmondsworth, UK: Penguin.

Winnicott, D. W. (1985). *The family and individual development.* London and New York: Tavistock Press.

Aspects of development and therapeutic work

Anderson, R. & Dartington, A. (Ed.). (1998). *Facing out: Clinical perspectives on adolescent disturbance.* London: Duckworth.

Boston, M. & Szur, R. (Ed.). (1983). *Psychotherapy with severely deprived children.* London: Routledge & Kegan Paul.

Bowlby, J. (1988). *A secure base: clinical applications of attachment theory.* London: Routledge.

Box, S. (Ed.). (1994) *Crisis at adolescence: Object/relations therapy with the family.* London: Jason Aronson.

Copley, B. (1993). *The world of adolescence: Literature, society and psychoanalytic psychotherapy.* London: Free Association Press.

Copley, B. & Forryan, B. (1997). *Therapeutic work with children and young people.* London: Cassell. (Original work published 1987.)

Lanyado, M. & Horne, A. (1999). *The handbook of child and adolescent psychotherapy: psychoanalytic approaches.* London: Routledge.

Laufer, M. (Ed.). (1997). *Adolescent breakdown and beyond.* London: Karnac.

Papadopoulos, R. K. & Byng-Hall, J. (Eds.). (1992). *Multiple voices: Narrative in systemic family psychotherapy.* London: Duckworth.

Trowell, J. & Bower, M. (Eds.). (1995). *The emotional needs of young children and their families.* London: Routledge.

Salzberger-Wittenberg, I. (1970). *Psychoanalytic insight and relationships: A Kleinian approach.* London: Routledge & Kegan Paul.

Szur, R. & Miller, L. (Eds.). (1991). *Extending horizons: psychoanalytic psychotherapy with children, adolescents and families.* London: Karnac.

Winkley, L. (1996). *Emotional problems in children and young people.* London: Cassell.

Observational studies

Briggs, S. (1997). *Growth and risk in infancy.* London: Jessica Kingsley.

Piontelli, A. (1992). *From foetus to child: An observational and psychoanalytic study.* London: Routledge.

Miller, L., Rustin, M. E., Rustin, M. J. and Shuttleworth, J. (1989). *Closely observed infants.* London: Duckworth.

Reid, S. (Ed.). (1977). *Developments in infant observation: The Tavistock model.* London: Routledge.

Relevant series of books

The Tavistock Series on Child Development (1992–95). London: Rosendale Press. A series of 16 books from *Understanding your baby* to *Understanding 18–20-year olds.*

Relevant theory

Anderson, R. (Ed.). (1992). *Clinical lectures on Klein and Bion.* London: Routledge.

Britton, R., Feldman, M. & O'Shaughnessy, E. (1989). *The Oedipus complex today: Clinical implications.* London: Karnac.

Freud, S. (1977). *The Pelican Freud library.* Harmondsworth, UK: Penguin.

Holmes, J. (1993). *John Bowlby and Attachment Theory.* London: Routledge.

Meltzer, D. (1978). *The Kleinian development.* Strath Tay, UK: Clunie Press.

Segal, H. (1988). *An introduction to the work of Melanie Klein* (2nd ed.). London: Karnac Books.

Symington, N. (1986). *The analytic experience.* London: Free Association Books.

Directory of further learning opportunities

We would like to thank Beta Copely and Barbara Forryan for giving permission to use and update this Directory, previously published in *Therapeutic work with children and young people*, Cassell, 1987 and 1997.

OPPORTUNITIES

Opportunities known to the authors at the time of publication which are likely to have a broadly similar conceptual basis to that of this book.

Courses in Observational Studies and the Application of Psychoanalytic Concepts to Work with Children, Young People, and Families

Various other courses may also be available at these addresses. *Enquiries to:*

Course Administrator,
Psychoanalytic Observational Studies Course, Academic Services,
Tavistock Clinic,
120 Belsize Lane,
London NW3 5BA, UK.

Organising Tutor,
Birmingham Trust for Psychoanalytic Psychotherapy,
96 Park Hill,
Moseley,
Birmingham B13 8DS, UK.

Organising Tutor,
UBHT Teaching Care,
Child and Adolescent Service, Knowle Clinic,

Broadfield Road,
Knowle,
Bristol BS4 2UH, UK.

Organising Tutor,
TSCYP, Scottish Institute of Human Relations,
13 Park Terrace,
Glasgow G3 6BY, UK.

Course Administrator,
Lincoln Centre and Institute of Psychotherapy,
19 Abbeville Mews,
88 Clapham Park Road,
London SW4 7BX, UK.

Course Administrator,
Leeds Community and Mental Health NHS Teaching Trust,
Southfield House,
Clarendon Road,
Leeds LS2 7PJ, UK.

Course Administrator,
Merseyside Psychotherapy Institute,
c/o Dept. Child and Adolescent Psychiatry, Alder Hey Children's Hospital,
Eaton Road,
Liverpool L12 2AP, UK.

Organising Tutor,
The Oxford Observation Course,
c/o 12 Rectory Road,
St. Clements,
Oxford OX4 1BW, UK.

Other varied opportunities

Enquiries to:

Consultant Child Psychotherapist,
North Devon Family Consultancy,
Barnstaple Health Centre,
Vicarage Street,
Barnstaple,
Devon EX32 7BT, UK.

Principal Child Psychotherapist,
Iddesleigh House,
Child Adolescent and Family Consultation Service,
97 Heavitree Road,
Exeter EX1 2NE, UK.

Senior Child Psychotherapist,
Herefordshire Psychoanalytic Psychotherapy Group,
Child, Adolescent and Family Guidance Centre,
Health Centre,
Gaol Street,
Hereford HR1 2HU, UK.

Director of Training,
Nottingham Psychotherapy Unit,
St. Ann's House,
114 Thorneywood Mount,
Nottingham NG3 2PZ, UK.

Head Child Psychotherapist,
Plymouth Child and Family Consultation Service,
Erme House, Mount Gould Hospital,
Plymouth,
Devon PL4 7QD, UK.

Course Director,
Winnicott Centre for Children and Families,
Torbay Hospital Annexe,
187 Newton Road,
Torbay TQ2 7AJ, UK.

Organising Tutor
Centre for Psychoanalytic Studies,
University of Kent,
Canterbury,
Kent CT2 7NZ, UK.

Organising Tutor,
Newham Child and Family Consultation,
84 West Ham Lane,
London E15 4PT, UK.

Course Director,
Child and Adolescent Analytic Psychotherapy,
Trinity College,
c/o 45 Ailesbury Road,
Dublin 4,
Ireland.

Index

Made in the USA
Monee, IL
16 August 2021

75830400R00125